Praise for
The Ready-to-Read, Ready-to-Count Handbook

"Savage's program optimistically and cheerfully teach how to instill confidence in young learners."
     —*Booklist* (American Library Association)

"Here is an instantaneous learning program containing specific directions for instruction in pre-reading skills, the three Rs, number concepts and a great deal more."   —*The Los Angeles Times*

"Great games for teaching letter sounds, as well as pre-reading skills. . . . This is a good book to recommend to parents of young children who are ready to read."   —*Instructor*

"Mixing fun with learning [for preschoolers] can be one of the best instruments parents can use. . . and [this book] explains all of the basics in a step-by-step road map designed to provide parents with ammunition to do that."   —*Chicago Defender*

"Teresa Savage displays the rare sensitivity of an expert teacher and a warm mother. If you're a parent and do the things she tells you to do, they will work, and you'll have a fascinating time being part of your child's intellectual growth."

—Siegfried E. Engelmann, author of
Teach Your Child to Read in 100 Easy Lessons
and creator of the DISTAR reading program

"From the beginning, you have a positive feeling that both you and your child will be successful. Love and happiness, from parent to child, flow through the book."

—Charlotte Lockhard
author of *Discover Intensive Phonics for Yourself*

"This encouraging guide is easy to read, comprehend, and implement. It should be required reading for all parents."

—Professor and former Dean Mildred B. Griggs
College of Education
University of Illinois at Urbana-Champaign

The
Ready-to-Read,
Ready-to-Count
Handbook

(Previously titled *The Chalkboard in the Kitchen*)

Teresa Savage

NEWMARKET PRESS · New York

First published in hardcover by Dodd, Mead & Company, Inc.
First Newmarket printing: August 1991.
Second Newmarket edition: March 2001.

01 02 03 04 05 10 9 8 7 6 5 4 3 2 1

The author gratefully acknowledges permission to reprint the following material:

Chapter 3, Game 6 (Biscuit Bake) and **Game 11** (Family Foot) adapted from *Thinking Is Child's Play* by Evelyn Sharp. Copyright © 1969 by Evelyn Sharp. Reprinted by permission of the publisher, E. P. Dutton, Inc.
Chapter 3, Game 15 (Chalkboard Jungle) and **Game 19** (Rhyme-Time) adapted from *School Before Six: A Diagnostic Approach* by L. Hogden and others, 1974, and reproduced by permission of the publisher, CEMREL, Inc., St. Louis, MO.
Chapter 3, Game 22 (Word Painting) adapted from *Games to Improve Your Child's English* by Abraham B. Hurwitz and Arthur Goddard. Copyright © 1970 by Abraham B. Hurwitz and Arthur Goddard. Reprinted by permission of the publisher, Simon & Schuster, a Division of Gulf & Western Corporation.
Chapter 8, Learning to Count, from *Preventing Failure in the Primary Grades* by Sigfried Engelmann. Copyright © 1969 by Science Research Associates, Inc. Adapted and reprinted by permission of the publisher.

Library of Congress Cataloging-in-Publication Data

Savage Teresa.
  [Chalkboard in the kitchen]
  The ready-to-read, ready-to-count handbook / Teresa Savage.
    p. cm.
  Reprint. Originally published: The chalkboard in the kitchen. New York : Dodd Mead, 1985.
  Includes bibliographical references and index.
  ISBN 1-55704-413-9 (pb) 1-55704-453-8 (hc)
  1. Early childhood education—Parent participation. 2. Reading (Preschool).
3. Creative activities and seat work. 4. Educational games.
I. Title.
LB1139.35.P37S38 1991
649'.68—dc20   91-12286
                                                      CIP

Quantity Purchases:

Companies, professional groups, and other organizations may qualify for special terms when ordering quantities of this title. For information, contact Special Sales, Newmarket Press, 18 East 48th Street, New York, NY 10017, (212) 832-3575 or (800) 669-3903, FAX (212) 832-3629, or e-mail mailbox@newmarketpress.com.

Manufactured in the United States of America.

Contents

INTRODUCTION

When I wrote *The Ready-to-Read, Ready-to-Count Handbook*, my children were barely out of preschool and ideas such as homeschooling, charter schools, and the Internet were barely visible on the horizon. Since then, new innovations and technologies have enriched our lives and given us access to more information and resources than ever before. With each new innovation has come challenges and opportunities as well as the need to reexamine old values in light of the new possibilities. Yet no matter how the cards of life and learning are reshuffled by each generation, certain truths remain. One is that parents are their children's first and most important teachers. The values, ideas, and ideals they instill in children at an early age become their foundation for the future and roadmap to future promise.

Over the years, *The Ready-to-Read, Ready-to-Count Handbook* has been used by thousands of parents to teach their children reading and math. The book's dual message of solid educational content coupled with old-fashioned values has stood the test of time and showed parents how to help their children become successful learners. Many parents have told me that the book's philosophy of learning with love makes it unique among educational books for parents.

I've received many gratifying letters and comments from parents all over the country, telling me how much my book has helped their children. One of my favorites is from a young mother whose experiences were similar to my own. Annie was married, in graduate school, and raising two preschoolers. She had wanted to put her four-year-old in a prestigious local preschool; but couldn't fit the cost of the school's tuition into the family budget. So instead, she went to the local bookstore in search of ideas and found my book. As she began practicing the teaching methods in *The Ready-to-Read, Ready-to-Count Handbook*, she found herself becoming more confident as a parent, and to her surprise, her son seemed to be enjoying his daily lessons with her.

Several months later when her son started to read books, she took him to a university preschool for gifted children for testing. Not only did he pass its battery of rigorous academic skills tests, but also the school awarded him a scholarship! Encouraged, Annie began to use the methods in *The Ready-to-Read, Ready-to-Count Handbook* with her young daughter, and she achieved the same success as her brother. Now both of Annie's children attend the university preschool for gifted children.

Many other parents have told me similar stories. Sometimes, it's a parent whose child was admitted into an Ivy League college or top engineering school. Sometimes, it's the parent of a child with learning disabilities who learned to read. After using my methods at home, my own son and daughter excelled in school and went on to receive academic scholarships from excellent universities.

Although I wrote *The Ready-to-Read, Ready-to-Count Handbook* with parents in mind, I have been surprised by the large numbers of teachers, child development specialists, and speech pathologists who've told me that they use the methods and ideas in my book with their students.

A great deal of research for the book came from the National Center for the Study of Reading and from interviewing many parents of successful children. More modern technologies and research methods have increased our understanding of how children learn and how the brain functions. New research from the National Institutes of Health (NIH) scientifically confirms why the teaching techniques discussed in *The Ready-to-Read, Read-to-Count Handbook* work so well.

Research indicates that the mastery of certain prerequisite skills is necessary for children to acquire language and learn to read. Before children can associate sounds with letters and blend sounds into words, as in phonics, children must be "phonemically aware." In other words, they must be able to hear and distinguish the individual sounds of the language (phonemes). Phonemic awareness forms the building blocks needed to acquire higher-order language and reading skills.

Further research indicates that early reading acquisition has a cumulative effect. Children who learn to read early tend to maintain this educational advantage throughout their school years. Studies also show that 20–25 percent of grade school children are deficit in phonemic awareness skills and will continue to lag behind in reading development without intervention training. This may explain why children who receive early training in reading and math usually continue to do well throughout middle and high school as well as college.

The Ready-to-Read, Ready-to-Count Handbook is an intensive training program that lays the bedrock foundation necessary for children to read well—phonemic awareness, phonological processing, and phonics reading instruction. Young learners master the prerequisite skills necessary for language and reading development through playful activities with no stress. Research from NIH and other research institutions support the book's reading and language arts methods as powerful educational tools.

Recently, I have become interested in the ways technology can be used to help teachers, parents, and childcare providers teach young children. My interests led me to co-found a company that uses CD-ROMs and distance-learning programs to help others teach, inform, and nurture young children. At Softchalk Learning Systems, Inc. (www.softchalklearning.com), our goal is to build an informational network that helps parents and teachers give the gift of learning with love to young children. I am very interested in hearing suggestions and ideas that have worked well for parents and teachers. You can e-mail me at teresa@softchalklearning.com, and I will pass them along. It is a privilege to be part of each child's success and I welcome your ideas. Together, we can give our young children wings.

To my children who made teaching a pleasure,
and to my mother who made learning a delight.

I am very grateful to the many parents, educators, and friends who gave so freely of their time and knowledge; however, I would especially like to thank Alvey Jones for his imaginative comic strip drawings; Siegfried Engelmann for teaching me how to teach; Lucie Spieler for her encouragement and editorial direction; and the staff of the University of Illinois Center for the Study of Reading for providing me with a wealth of information.

I would also like to thank Barbara Turner for suggesting I write this book.

ONE

A Gift of Wings

Motherhood is a curious paradox. We give birth and unlock a limitless potential in our child, yet we seldom appreciate the reservoir of potential we unlock in ourselves.

We guide stubby fingers that can't hold slippery soap into dexterity. We translate a complex code of coos, cries, babbles, and gurgles into language. We show wobbly limbs that once floated how to carry weight and shoulder responsibility. We cure insecurity with a smile, we treat failure with compassion, and we return effort with encouragement. But for all our instruction, we never think of ourselves as teachers.

True, our lessons don't come with checkmarks, chalkboards, bell schedules, or paychecks, and our professional credentials are more likely to impress a circus acrobat than a board of examiners; but nonetheless, we are accomplished teachers who develop our techniques on the daily routine of motherhood and we teach lessons of life and love that last a lifetime.

Unfortunately, only a few mothers have the time, the resources, and the faith in their own maternal instincts to perfect this potential. These rare women nurture, nudge, and carry out this primary role of mother as teacher with the thoroughness and singleness of purpose of a wise robin preparing her brood for flight.

But for most of us, this early kinship in learning is a fleeting relationship—peaking at toilet training and petering out soon afterward. Instead of expanding our teaching horizons we unwittingly settle into the second-status role of the butcher, the baker, the chauffeur, and go-fer and fritter away the time and opportunity to give our children a legacy of learning that can determine the heights to which they later soar.

And we fail our children *not* because we're lazy, incapable, or unconcerned, but quite frankly because no one has ever told us exactly how best to teach our children and then given us permission to do it.

The educational community could tell parents precisely how and what to teach, but contrary to evidence that many parents have successfully taught preschoolers reading, writing, and arithmetic, and that these lessons have resulted in permanent educational gains, the typical educator's knee-jerk response to any parent who pursues the subject of home teaching is don't.

The few learning programs available for parental use either fail to teach or are purposely weighted down with additional exercises to increase cost; or were designed by educational psychologists and written as though it is perfectly normal for a four-year-old to bark and salivate at a blinking light.

The child-care books from the cater-to-your kid books that categorize a whack on the bottom as assault and battery, down through the back-to-the-country books that prescribe pre-penicillin practices, all tell more about caring for your child's body than about developing his mind.

Consequently, many parents who might teach are often discouraged by lack of information or fear of being labelled "pushy"; and those parents who do teach are as hushed-up about it as about their safe-deposit box number.

I began teaching my son how to read and compute math a few months after his fourth birthday. I did it for a couple of conscientious, rational reasons, and a few sentimental, self-indulgent reasons.

Like many parents I had begun to question the effectiveness of a public school system that was plagued by teacher strikes, bankruptcy, declining reading levels, and teacher burnout; but I was also faced with the grim reality that although I was middle class in the cultural sense, I had no extra money for the private schooling, tutors, and expensive home in a "good" school district that would have ensured a quality education for my child.

In my home, television had become a kind of video narcotic and I watched in dismay as my preschooler rapidly became a boob-tube junkie who skipped meals and ignored friends and family just to get that electronic fix.

Beyond that, and for purely self-indulgent reasons, I wanted to snatch a few quiet moments away from the scouring and scolding and give my son a special gift, a gift of knowledge that would be both a launching point and a learning foundation. I wanted him to find the friends, the humor, the pathos, and the history of humanity in books, and to find them with the same joy, pride, approval, and applause he had known when he took his first steps.

Unfortunately, my beautiful gift languished in the delivery. The incessant demands of running a household, my own disorganization and lack of direction, and the gnawing insecurity that I might be doing something wrong, all kept me from accomplishing my goal sooner.

Finally, the how-tos of my gift came into sharp focus the winter morning I got a call from a nearby laboratory school to substitute teach. The elementary school was affiliated with a prestigious teacher education university and the only state supported lab school of its kind in Illinois. The school had an excellent reputation and the student body was, for the most part, the children of the university's faculty.

Three years earlier on a post-partum whim I had called up the school, placed my name on the substitute list, and then forgotten about the incident. Apparently, they had forgotten about me as well, that is, until a record-breaking blizzard prevented half of the regular staff from coming to work that morning.

Although I had previously taught elementary school I hadn't worked outside the home since I had gotten married and started raising a family, and ordinarily, I would have said no to a substitute teaching position.

But that particular snow-laden morning both my two-year-old and my four-year-old were healthy and energetic beyond my endurance, and the prospect of teaching twenty-five strangers from a safe distance was not as unsettling as living with two overly familiar faces up close.

When I arrived at the school I found my sixth-grade class exceptionally bright, resourceful, well-behaved, and several grade levels above the national average in all subjects. The class breezed through assignment after assignment and by lunchtime completed what would have normally been considered an entire day's work. The curriculum and the textbooks were the traditional ones found in thousands of classrooms throughout the country and I was somewhat puzzled how this seemingly typical American classroom produced atypical students. It wasn't until later that afternoon that I got my answer.

The regular teacher had left an extra-credit Social Studies assignment which included a class discussion on the family as a socialization agent. As the discussion progressed and we moved from the textbook example to real life situations, student after student attributed his educational gains to having been taught reading and math by a parent before kindergarten.

They said when they were just toddlers their parents had used their educational expertise to devise educational games that the whole family played and enjoyed. Many of the students said their parents were still actively teaching them academic subjects after school hours and some students felt this one-on-one instruction was the most meaningful and fun they had ever known.

What a revelation! I had gone to the school to teach the lesson and I was the one who learned. Imagine, many of the college professors who determine teacher education curriculum, and who publicly advise parents to leave the teaching to the schools, privately teach their children at home—and apparently with great success. I wondered what elementary school teachers would say about pushy parents if they knew this!

Right then and there I made up my mind that somehow or

other I would find ways to give my children the same educational advantage, even if it meant getting rid of my antique china cabinet and putting up a chalkboard in my kitchen.

I spent the next few months talking to mothers of successful children, interviewing college professors about the at-home application of their learning theories, and talking to children about school.

I reviewed old textbooks and read all the newest ones on education. I studied books on sociology and psychology. Again and again certain principles emerged and I began to practice them in an at-home teaching program with my four-year-old with great success.

Almost immediately I noticed changes in my son, Benjamin. It was as if a whole new world had opened up for him and for me. He began to discover the letters of the alphabet in everything: newspapers, magazines, traffic signs, grocery store logos. He delighted in his own imagination where broken twigs were v's, chairs were h's, carrots with the tops attached were dotted i's, and the whistling of the wind was the sound of the letter w.

His speech became clearer, more complex, and more deliberate. He kicked the television habit and started watching more educational programs and fewer recreational ones. He developed an insatiable appetite for books and I knew we had crossed a major hurdle in learning and in values the day he broke his piggy bank and used his hard-earned savings to purchase a dinosaur book rather than the previously desired cap pistol.

And at four and a half, only a few months after I turned my kitchen into a classroom, Benjamin began to read.

There were other changes too, subtle changes that are never measured by an achievement or intelligence test, but nevertheless changes that were equally as valid as the intellectual gains.

My son became gentler with and more tolerant of his younger sister. He was easier to discipline and reason with. He seemed happier with himself and was less frustrated by failure. He became more positive and self-confident and he had the tangible reality of accomplishment to back up those attitudes. But perhaps most important, he began to see success as the

8

consequence of hard work and the mastery of specific skills rather than a haphazard, elusive, and random occurrence.

Others noticed the difference as well. My husband thinks both his wife and son are brilliant, and the teaching of our children has become a delightful shared family activity. The grandparents tell me how well-adjusted and bright my children are and they applaud me for putting the next generation on solid footing. Even our sixteen-year-old babysitter asked me to write down some of my methods so she could use them with her younger brothers and sisters.

I have shared my program with a number of interested friends and they have reported successful results as well. None of these mothers is a trained teacher, but each one loved her child enough to give a special gift of time, of love, and of herself.

Now let's talk a little about this book: the program outlined in this book is for anyone who felt there was a sharp discrepancy between the tremendous amount of time and instruction devoted to preparing parents for the baby's arrival and a small amount of time and instruction devoted to preparing parents for the baby's departure. It is for any woman who seeks an alternative to a "liberated" doctrine that insists motherhood is dull and tiresome. It is for parents who want their children to be good students even though the educational system is often inhumane and ineffectual. In fact, although I address this book to mothers and use a male child as a student, this book can be used by anyone who spends a fair amount of time with a child and who wants to be a full participant in that child's early education.

The Ready-to-Read, Ready-to-Count Handbook is unique in that it is two books combined into one: a teacher's training manual for parents and an activity workbook for children. Each chapter contains *assignments* for the parent to master and *lessons* for the parent to teach the child, and it's wise to read through the entire book before you teach the lessons, to learn what is expected of you and to learn what you can realistically expect of your child.

Chapter Two shows you how to bring love and sensitivity into your at-home classroom by accenting the positive, and it is essentially an initiation into effective and responsive teaching skills.

Chapter Three uses games which everyone in the family can enjoy to teach your child coordination, logic, listening, and direction skills.

Chapter Four is a beginning reading program that uses a reading comic strip to teach children as young as three years old the sounds of the alphabet and how to read.

Chapters Five through Seven continue the reading comic strip and the reading program and show you how to help your child painlessly progress from reading words to reading books.

Chapter Eight is a basic math program based upon games, activities, and creative problem solving.

I have found the rewards of becoming an active participant in my child's education more pleasurable than a cashmere sweater, more exciting than a trip to the Rose Bowl, and more wholesome than home-baked bread. And so will you. And maybe, just maybe, those of us who put the chalkboard in the kitchen give our children the best gift of all—wings.

TWO
Let It Begin With Me

The idea of mother as teacher is not a new concept. Years before warranties, ready mix, Big Macs, and Betty Crocker, skills and trades were passed down from mother to daughter and from father to son. However, the traditional role of parent as teacher got snagged in the gears of the industrial revolution and was tossed out the window as unceremoniously as a paper towel. Anthropologist Margaret Mead duly noted, "Our children were the first generation who had nothing practical to learn from their parents' and grandparents' experience in life."

Fortunately, we can overcome this feeling of parental impotence and you can become your child's best and most effective teacher even if you flunked *Romper Room*, have lost *Mother Goose*, or would rather show a preschooler how to dial out for a pizza than how to bake one. No matter.

Almost any adult who has patience and the desire to give can provide the educational skills that are vital for her child's intellectual growth and development. And there is no secret formula either. Many of the same principles that make for good mothering also make for good teaching; and perhaps without knowing it, you have successfully used basic principles of education and psychology in your everyday routine.

Now with some help you're going to hone those techniques, take some of the trial and error out, and add a few tricks to your repertoire. But first you must clear your mind of the rhetoric that says, "I can't" or "I shouldn't," because whether or not you're up to the job, you are your child's first and most important teacher. And once you relax and accept this challenge you can appreciate some of the advantages parents who teach have over "the experts."

- You already have laid a foundation for learning. Each time you and your child bake cookies, go for a walk, play pat-a-cake, discuss a story, or kiss good-night, you are shaping and influencing that child's behavior.
- You already love your child. He doesn't have to win a gold star or bring home a trophy to win your love. Your love is constant and unconditional.
- You respect his intelligence. You've seen your child inspect a caterpillar with the patient curiosity of a biologist, you've marveled at his use of deductive reasoning to locate a missing sock, and you've heard his closing arguments for a later bedtime. You know your kid is smart.
- You have a long-term investment in his education. Unlike his teacher at school, you are not just responsible for getting him through one grade and on to another, you're responsible for providing the skills and continuity to get him through life.
- Your student teacher ratio is one-to-one, not 25:1, and one-on-one teaching is a fun, effective, and exhilarating process that nourishes the learner and replenishes the teacher.

Now let's put away those feelings of inadequacy and get down to the business of learning how to teach.

In this chapter we will concentrate on the skills that will help make you, your child's first teacher, his best teacher. You will learn how to identify, organize, and build those skills you already possess into an effective teaching program. You'll understand why a teaching program that's generous with praise and kisses is more effective (and fun) than one that is peppered with criticism and disapproval. You'll start a language center and I'm convinced once you understand the teaching potential of pictures you'll collect junk mail with the same enthusiasm you would fifty-cents-off coupons.

But before you embark on this program I should warn you that some of the assignments may seem unusual or make you feel uncomfortable. That's only because you're not accustomed to seeing them in a teaching context. Simply approach them with the same adventurous spirit you would a new gourmet recipe, a wickedly expensive French perfume, or your best friend's herbal blend for dry skin. And I bet once you finish reading this chapter and start practicing the assignments, you will not only have laid the foundation for a brighter child, but you'll have built the framework for a more loving and open relationship.

PUT LOVE IN YOUR TEACHING PLAN

There are specific ways to put love into your teaching plan, and even though it's unlikely you will find the next five assignments in a teacher's training manual, I'm convinced they are the most important assignments in this book. These assignments aren't valuable because they are guaranteed to produce super-tots, brainy babies, or raise intelligence quotients; but they are invaluable because they do something more important—they raise your and your child's capacity to give and receive love and they create the emotional climate for learning to flourish.

Assignment #1. Love Quota

As parents, much of our preoccupation with our children's needs centers around quotas. There are nutritional quotas, class size quotas, intelligence quotas, but even though we know children need (and like) to be hugged, kissed, and cuddled, no one ever talks about love quotas. Psychologists tend to shy away from setting a fixed amount on parental affection and say it depends upon the child and the situation. If you ask your child how many kisses he wants you're likely to get an answer similar to the one I got from my son, "ten thousand kisses a day."

Your first assignment is designed to help you determine the amount of affection you give your child and to evaluate the quality of that affection.

For three consecutive days I want you to log the number of times you show affection toward your child and record the times you kiss, hug, cuddle, and say words of endearment such as: I love you, you're a terrific person, I'm lucky to have you for my child, etc. After you complete your log, look for patterns of affection and if you spot any weak points, here are a few simple ways to be a more demonstrative and loving parent:

1. Do you kiss only at bedtime or good-byes? If so, your affection may seem more perfunctory than sincere. Try to be more impromptu and less predictable.

2. Do you tell your child you love him or her at least once a day? Do you ever say why? Parent/child relationships, just like husband/wife relationships, don't just happen—they require work. If you haven't recently told your child just how special he or she is, why don't you, along with the other members of the family, get together and tell that child just how terrific you think he or she is.

3. Do you hug, kiss, or cuddle your child at least four times a day? Social scientist Virginia Satir insists that four hugs a day are necessary to survive, eight hugs are needed for maintenance, and twelve hugs are necessary for growth. Even though I realize you can't dole out affection as you would a vitamin C tablet, and that there is no magic number specifying how much affection your child needs, I know you can't have a healthy parent/child relationship or pupil/teacher relationship without affection. My experience is that kids crave affection and if you kiss, hug, and cuddle each day and

LOVE QUOTA LOG

Time of affection	Kiss	Hug	Cuddle	Words of endearment

give extra doses on those days of skinned knees, fights with friends, and lost pets, you'll be taking an important step toward establishing a relationship based upon love and acceptance.

Some parents will have already established a dialogue of love between themselves and the child, and may find this exercise unnecessary; but most of us let physical affection slide bit by bit, particularly as the child gets older.

The talk show host Phil Donahue once revealed on his TV show that he regretted not being more affectionate toward his sons when they were younger. Phil said he has since become more affectionate, but now when he tries to hug or kiss, the teenagers react as though they were taking a cold shower. But he still tries, and you must too, every day.

These daily doses of love are your way of letting your child know how special he is to you regardless of whether he wiggles in his seat, confuses 9s and 6s, gives the wrong answer, or sings off key.

Assignment #2. Echo Listening

Good parenting and good teaching involve hugs, squeezes, kisses, words of endearment, and more—understanding. Perhaps even the frustrated teenager's litany, "Yeah, I know my folks *love* me, but they don't understand me!" began twelve years earlier when a frustrated two-year-old unintelligibly mumbled the same thing. This feeling of not being understood is a storm cloud on the learning-with-love course you are charting and there is a counseling technique I'll call echo listening that can bring sensitivity to your at-home classroom.

Echo listening is the practice of restating the problem or concern of the child in your own words so that the child hears back his own complaint restated by you. It is a technique used by psychologists in counseling sessions and the technique is taught in Parent Effectiveness Training Classes. A good echo listening session dissolves tensions, opens the channels for communication, strikes a chord of camaraderie between parent and child, and clears the air for some kind of solution.

Here's how echo listening works:

Child: "Derek said he hates me."

Mother: "Derek said he doesn't like you?"

Child: "Yeah, he said I broke his racing car and he doesn't want to be my friend anymore."

Mother: "So you broke Derek's car and now he's angry?"

Child: "I didn't mean to. I was playing with it and the door fell off."

Mother: "It was an accident."

Child: "Uh-huh." (Silence)
"Can you fix it for me?"

Mother: "Sure, go bring me some glue."
(Child goes off to find glue.)

Although solutions to problems often accompany echo listening, the resolution of conflict is not the primary goal. The goal of echo listening is the cathartic process of releasing feelings and sharing concerns with an empathetic listener; and interestingly enough, the talker will often arrive at his own solutions.

The overall effect echo listening has on your teaching program is that it legitimizes the child's point of view and provides a safety valve that allows the child to freely say when the work is too hard or confusing.

Your second assignment is to practice echo listening with your husband or some other adult to get a feel for how the technique works. After you've rehearsed it a couple of times, try it with your child the next time he or she comes to you with a problem.

Assignment #3. Shared Time

Your child needs to know he has access to you at times other than "school times" or "troubled times" and it is these quiet moments of shared time that provide the mortar to sustain the relationship through the uncertainties that are bound to come with any new learning venture. This time should be unstructured and make no demand upon either you or the child to be clever, cute, original, or bright. It is just time to grow and share.

Assignment #3 is to set aside fifteen minutes each day to share time with your child.

Assignment #4. Get Dad Involved

Although I personally know one Superdad who believes "woman's work" is the same as "man's work" (he diapers bottoms, helps with housework, mixes formula, understands the intricacies of the rectal thermometer, and may well go on to become the first homeroom mother with hairy underarms!), he is clearly the exception and most of us don't have husbands like him.

As a matter of fact, reliable sources say the average father spends only a few minutes each week playing with his child. That's less time than television viewing, yardwork, or a commute into the city. Imagine, a lot of dads out there are on better terms with their shower massage than their four-year-old!

Traditionally this sorry situation has been blamed on everything from a sexist corporate structure to a hormonal imbalance to a bad toss. It's as though we psychologically bury the father/child relationship early in the game and dig it up years later when junior wants a driver's license.

But sometimes you can get around this. It's not always easy, but it's not impossible either. And the increased likelihood of a fuller, richer, family life is more than worth the effort.

Assignment #4 is to get your husband interested and involved in the teaching of the child. Some of you will find this easier than others and here are some suggestions for getting the "reluctant father" involved in the early education of his child:

1. Keep a diary of the various games and activities you and your child have played and especially enjoyed. Record your feelings at the moment and include notes about special impressions and reactions. When your husband has had time to eat and relax, share your notes with him. He might even get interested enough to share in the fun the next day. (Don't throw these notes away, they'll make great conversation pieces years later.)

2. Set aside one evening each week (Mondays seem to work best for many families) for family play and shared activities. The idea is to turn off the television and to turn each other on. The activities could be board games, magic shows, art projects, or any games that suit your family's particular interests. (On family night try to prepare a high protein and low carbohydrate dinner. If you cook potatoes, spaghetti, cakes, and breads, you'll be too exhausted to participate and everyone else will be snoring by the time you finish cleaning up the kitchen.)

3. Be patient and flexible and don't try to pressure your husband into participating. If he won't participate this Monday, try him a week from now.

Now that you're aware of showing affection for your child and spending time with him, let's talk about some ways to give him an atmosphere of encouragement in which to learn.

Assignment #5. Accent the Positive

Positive reinforcement is the use of positive feedback to change behavior. It is a technique used by teachers to manage classrooms, by industry to keep workers on-task, by behavior modificationists to help dieters lose weight, and it can be used by you to help your child learn. To get a general idea how positive reinforcement works, let's conduct our own offbeat version of a well-known magazine's column, "Can This Marriage Be Saved?" Here's the scenario . . .

> It's a typical disorganized afternoon at your home. The house is a wreck, the kids are still in pajamas, dinner is in the thawing-out stage, and your hair looks as though it was styled with an egg beater. Just as you're about to wash down two aspirins with a little cooking sherry . . . enter . . . THE HUSBAND. Home from work early and unexpected.

Would you prefer your husband to . . .

A. Describe in detail what he sees.
B. Lecture you on the finer points of housekeeping.
C. Glance at the thawing hamburger and cheerfully carol, "Great, you've started dinner!"

Of course any man who has the bad taste to come home early and unexpected deserves to be thrown out along with the dinner; but for the sake of this argument and your marriage, let's say you choose C. Quite simply, no one wants to hear the bad stuff, not even when it's as plain as the dust on the furniture or the fingerprints on the refrigerator. And any lecturer intent upon pointing out the bad to the exclusion of the good will most likely find his lesson falling on deaf and ungrateful ears.

Although accenting the positive will do for starters to improve the quality of your relationships, the gist of positive reinforcement is not only to recognize good, but to follow the good with a reward. Psychologists and educators have developed specific steps to apply positive reinforcement to learning situations.

1. *Identify the goal.* Let's say you want your preschooler to be a good reader. That's a nice idea, but it's too general and nonspecific to really qualify as a goal. Goals should be written

in terms of performance and a better goal would be one that is measurable and clarifies the objective. An example of a goal is, "I want my preschooler to read at a first-grade level of competency by age six." This last goal places boundaries on what is and what is not expected (a first-grade level of reading competency); sets a time limit on when the performance is expected (by age six); and is specific enough to be tested for (use of standardized tests).

2. *List the goal's related behaviors.* This takes a little research because you'll need to compile a list of the behaviors and skills that lead to your particular goal. If your goal is to get your child reading at a first-grade level of competency by age six then you'll need to find out which prereading and reading skills and behaviors are involved. You can obtain this kind of information from the head of curriculum instruction at your local school district, the state commissioner of education, teacher training manuals available at public or university libraries, or from some of the references listed in Appendix 1. After you complete your research you should have a list of skills to teach as well as a list of specific behaviors to observe for.

3. *Identify and list the rewards.* In order to make sure your reward is a powerful reinforcer your child will work for, you'll need to find out what his particular preferences are. If you don't take time either to ask or observe what your child likes best you may find that "marvelous" toy you've chosen makes him about as happy as a secretary with a new bottle of correction fluid. My own teaching experience indicates that tangible rewards that can be consumed right on the spot such as candy, bits of fruit, raisins, M and M's, and peanuts work well with children three to eight years old. Social rewards such as hugs, applause, giving five, and kisses are also big incentives, particularly when the giver is Mom or Dad. Of course you'll need to find out which combination of tangible and social rewards works best for your child.

4. *Reinforce immediately and after every response made toward the goal.* Every single time your child makes the response you want, reward him—immediately! Don't wait. Let him eat that jelly bean right now. It only takes a minute and you'll be amazed at how fast and eagerly kids learn when there is something in it for them besides a lecture.

In the book *How To Discipline with Love* Dr. Fitzhugh Dodson tells the story of a psychologist who used positive reinforcement to teach wild bears how to play basketball. Each time the bears moved toward the basketball hoop the psychologist would reward them with a piece of meat.

Of course at first the bears didn't have the slightest idea how to play basketball, but they did eventually figure out that when they approached the hoop, they got something good. By using the same principle the psychologist was later able to get the bears to shoot baskets and retrieve balls.

As the mother of two active preschoolers I know there are days when children seem grumpier and more disagreeable than bears and it's hard to find anything positive to reward. If you have days like this too, wait until you and your child are in better moods, or ask a friend, spouse, or the child's grandmother to conduct the teaching session. Grandmothers are especially good teachers because they can usually find something good to say about the rascal even when Mama's so mad she's seeing red.

5. *Pair the reinforcer with the desirable behavior.* The moment your child does what you want, give him the reward and say why. For example: "I'm clapping because you picked up that book" . . . "Here's a big hug for that good talking" . . . "You get a raisin because you're paying attention."

Never say, "If you sit quietly, I'll give you a cookie." That's a bribe and the minute you start bribing you lose control over the learning situation and stop determining the child's behavior and he starts determining your behavior. The result is that the reinforcement gets reversed and you could end up with a kid who won't be happy with anything less than the keys to a Honda.

6. *Ignore every response except the one you want.* Ignoring undesirable behavior is the most important step in positive reinforcement and it is also the step where parents typically make the most mistakes. Apparently many a parent's approach to mobilizing little Johnny into action means more "shouting it out" and less "waiting it out." Unfortunately, besides the strained larynx, we pay another price for this temporary release: children who habitually receive more attention for being bad than for being good actually increase the frequency of the undesirable (bad) behavior.

Kids figure any attention is better than no attention and parents who show concern only when the child misbehaves actually reward the bad behavior by giving it attention and punish the good behavior by ignoring it.

The implication for your teaching program is that if you want your child to acquire the skills and behaviors related to the goal you've identified, you'll need to spend more time rewarding the behavior you like and less time reprimanding the behavior you don't like.

Dr. Wesley Becker, a former professor of mine and author of *Parents Are Teachers*, says, "Catch the children being good, rather than bad."

Fortunately, catching kids being good doesn't mean standing there muffling screams while little Sara unravels the planter, and there are a few devices that make ignoring the bad more tolerable and finding the good more likely.

- Lower the requirements for rewards. Let's say you want your child to sit quietly and pay attention, but he's only sitting quietly. Reward him for sitting quietly and say why. He'll soon pay attention and when he does, give a reward.
- Create a diversion. Enthusiasm is contagious and when

you're animated, excited, and eager to teach, it's hard for your child to resist participating too.

- Tell him precisely what it is you want. Give brief instructions such as, "Eyes on board" . . . "Repeat after me" . . . "Listen closely" . . . and each time the child responds appropriately, give a reward.
- Stack the deck and make it easier for the child to learn than not to learn. One mother I spoke with wanted to divert her daughter's attention away from TV and into more mind-stimulating areas. The mother unplugged the TV and scattered magnets, metal objects, and science books around the house. Every time the girl would pick up a book or object the mother would hug, kiss, or applaud and say how happy she was about her daughter's interest in science. By the end of the afternoon session the two had conducted several experiments and were making plans to try more the next day.

Caution: if ignoring the bad means someone is in physical danger, *forget* about the bad and do something *fast*!!!

7. *Gradually reduce rewarding every response.* After your child gets a feel for how positive reinforcement works you won't need to reward every response. Perhaps you'll decide to reward every other response or choose to substitute social rewards for some of the tangible rewards, it's up to you. However, don't make the mistake of eliminating the reward altogether because when you remove the reinforcer you extinguish or eliminate the desired behavior.

Here's an example of how positive reinforcement works in a typical lesson. Let's take the game called Follow-the-Arrow from Chapter Three.

STEP 1.   *Identify and list the goal.*
Goal: For the child to play the game Follow-the-Arrow with and without assistance from teacher (mother).

STEP 2.   *List related behavior and skills.*
Sitting quietly while Mama explains.
Repeating the phrase, "The arrow goes this way."
Directioning with finger left to right.
Racing a toy car down the arrow, left to right.

STEP 3.   *Identify the reinforcers.*
Place a bowl of raisins, nuts, and pineapple chunks near the demonstration and be prepared to hug, smile, and kiss the child (when he gives the desired response).

STEP 4.   *Reinforce every response made toward the goal.*
Get the child's attention—reward.
Start explaining the lesson and as you demonstrate, reward the child immediately when he exhibits any of the behaviors in Step 2.

STEP 5.   *Pair the reward with a brief explanation why the reward is being given.*
Say, "I'm clapping because you raced the car down that arrow" . . . "Here's a big hug because you showed me the way the arrow goes."

And it's that easy, really.

There is controversy about whether reinforcement techniques should be used in learning situations. Some people feel the pursuit of education is reward in itself and anything additional the child receives for doing what is normally expected is a bribe. Others argue that children who seem motivated by the cerebral are actually responding to the social reinforcers of teacher approval, high grades, gold stars, etc. My opinion is that while the pursuit of education does seem to be reward enough for some children, for other children it simply isn't enough. First, most children don't understand or even care that the point of learning games such as Follow-the-Arrow is to teach left-to-right orientation, a skill crucial to reading. All the child knows is that Follow-the-Arrow is a game Mama likes to play.

Secondly, in the real world adults get paid for work in the form of paychecks, bonuses, paid vacations, and health benefits, and a child in school or at home learning can be legitimately seen as a worker.

Thirdly, learning is not always fun. Sometimes learning is hard, confusing, or downright boring and positive reinforcement is one way to reward effort and improvement.

Assignment #5 is to use positive reinforcement in an actual teaching situation with your child and play (Follow-the-Arrow, Game 2 in Chapter Three) with your child. In the beginning you'll need to reward even the smallest steps that lead to the goal, and to do this successfully you'll need to set aside an afternoon away from the distraction of the TV, the telephone, other children and household responsibilities to devote time to working with your child.

PREPARING THE CLASSROOM

Well, you've learned the script, rehearsed your cues, polished your performance, so now let's talk about the props and scenery.

Assignment #6. Materials

At a time when everyone in education seems to be crying out for more funds, more enrichment programs, and more supplies, I think you'll be pleasantly surprised to find out how well parents can teach with *less*. The essential, most important, cannot-teach-without, materials are:

A Chalkboard
Chalk—white and colored
Eraser

That's it—really. The use of a slate and stylus dates back to the ancients and it's no coincidence that in an era of computers, video-cassettes, and satellites, chalkboards are still the cornerstone of every modern classroom.

You can find a basic 18 in. by 24 in. chalkboard at variety stores, teacher supply stores, department stores, toy stores, and even some drug stores. The one I use cost less than five dollars and it came with chalk, eraser, and mounting hooks.

If you like, you can buy chalk paint at hardware stores or paint stores and paint the lower half of a wall with it. When the child outgrows need for the chalkboard you can paint over the chalkboard surface with regular paint. Caution: Before you paint, check the proper procedure with your local hardware or paint dealer.

The Language Center. The second most important teaching aid you need is an abundant supply of pictures. Most of teaching is visual and you can help your child speak, think, and write about his environment more clearly and effectively if you use pictures to start a Language Center. Essentially, a Language Center is a collection of pictures clipped from magazines, catalogs, junk mail, Sunday newspaper supplements, and other printed materials. You'll be using these pictures in many reading and language activities and so look for 3 in. by 5 in. or larger, multi-color pictures with these kinds of qualities: 1) pictures of rhyming subjects (e.g., mop, top, pop; fox, box; etc.), 2) pictures of objects that can be grouped by category (e.g., animals, furniture, food, vehicles, clothes, etc.), 3) pictures of objects that begin with the same sound (e.g., man, monkey, milk, etc.).

For easy access organize the pictures alphabetically or by category and keep your Language Center in a special container such as a box, drawer, or file cabinet. You may want to paste a cardboard backing onto some of the pictures for more durability or you might consider making a separate Language Center for your child's personal use.

Think of collecting pictures the same way you think of clipping store coupons. Always be alert to new sources of pictures and don't use the same pictures over and over any more than you'd try to redeem the same store coupon again and again.

Tactile Letter Cards. The more you involve a child's senses in the learning process, the greater his chances are for retaining information. And as you become more proficient in your role as teacher, you'll discover any number of imaginative ways to make learning a total sensory experience. One effective and easy way to include the sense of touch in an at-home reading program is to make a set of tactile letter cards.

Tactile letter cards are a variation of the Montessori sandpaper letters and they are essentially a set of felt or sandpaper letters affixed onto a cardboard base. They let a child feel the varying shapes of the letters and help him discriminate visually between vowels and consonants. To make a set for your child you'll need:

felt
sandpaper
stencils
scissors
glue
twenty-six 2 in. by 4 in. cardboard rectangles
or twenty-six index cards

The vowel letters are made from felt. To make a set for the vowels a, e, i, o, u, trace vowel stencils (or a pattern you've made yourself) onto felt. Cut out and glue the felt letters, smooth side up, onto an index card or cardboard rectangle.

The consonant letters are made from sandpaper. To make a set for the consonant sounds b, c, d, f, g, h, j, k, l, m, n, p, qu, r, s, t, v, w, x, y, and z, trace consonant stencils (or your own pattern) onto sandpaper. Cut out and glue the sandpaper letters, rough side up, onto an index card or cardboard rectangle.

Paper. Of course it almost goes without saying that you'll need a supply of paper and you can get paper at reasonable prices from discount stores, teachers' bookstores, and office supply stores. Some budget-minded mothers have made arrangements with local typists to buy their throwaways. One of the best sources of cheap cardboard is empty cereal boxes.

Your sixth assignment for this chapter is to get together your teaching supplies. That includes getting a chalkboard, chalk, and eraser; starting a Language Center; and making tactile alphabet cards.

Assignment #7. The Classroom

When I first started teaching I held class at the kitchen table. At the time we lived in a small apartment with an eat-in kitchen and I had cleared out some shelves and cabinets, and propped my chalkboard between the spice rack and the Campbell's soup. Perhaps to visitors my chalkboard looked incongruous nestled among the cans and canisters, but I never felt that way. To me it belonged right there in my kitchen because I knew the lessons I taught there nourished my children's minds, just as much as the food prepared there nourished their bodies.

Of course you don't literally have to put a chalkboard in your kitchen to teach your lessons. If you have the additional space of a sewing room, library, spare bedroom, or solarium, you could do as my friend Ann did and furnish it with miniature chairs and tables, chalkboard and chalk, books and bookshelves, file cabinets, and writing and art supplies. However, more important than the luxuriance of your facility is the need to establish a permanent storage area for your material and to develop a habit of holding class in one particular place.

Assignment #7 is to set aside a room or designate a special place to hold class and put your teaching materials in.

TIME TIPS

So far I've given you seven assignments and if you're like most busy mothers I bet you're wondering if you get seven extra hours a day to do them all in. Well, I can't concoct a thirty-one-hour day, but I can share with you some time tips that I've found helpful in organizing and using time more effectively.

1. Write a schedule of your typical day. Look for lulls of time when you and your child are preoccupied by expendable activities such as TV viewing, telephone conversations, etc. Many mothers find the ideal time to hold class is after breakfast or before afternoon naps. Working mothers might find the time after dinner and before bathtime best.

2. Hold class for a predetermined length of time. Depending upon the child's age and attention span, a fifteen- to thirty-minute session five days per week seems best. If you feel you need more time to cover a concept, you can hold additional three- to five-minute mini-sessions throughout the day.

3. Get into the habit of making things-to-do lists. A basic principle of time management is to make daily things-to-do lists according to A, B, and C priority. A lists have top priority and must be done today. B lists are necessary things-to-do, but not crucial. C lists are of least importance and can be done after the projects on the A and B lists are completed.

4. Delegate responsibility to other members of the family. Four-year-olds can learn to make beds and set the dinner table. Three-year-olds can pick up toys and turn off lights. Husbands, under the threat of desertion, can cook dinner or do laundry.

5. Plan weekly dinner menus. I started planning weekly menus to save money and found out it saved me time as well. I plan the menus on the weekends and include one meal that can be made in large quantities and freeze half for use the following week.

6. Plan your telephone time. When the telephone rang, I used to feel obligated to answer. Not any more. I've found out that telephone calls during a lesson break the continuity of the teaching and are unfair to the child. Now when I teach I lower the ring on the phone and if there is a natural break in the lesson I'll answer it. You can also take it off the hook, invest in an answering service, or tell your friends not to call at certain hours.

7. Be flexible. If you can't teach five days a week, settle for three or two. Children have fantastic memories and if you review the last concept covered before proceeding on to new ones they retain much of what you taught.

Assignment #8 is to designate a certain time each day, five days a week for class.

SUMMARY OF ASSIGNMENTS FOR CHAPTER TWO

1. Complete a Love Quota Log and work on improving any weak points.

2. Practice Echo Listening with an adult and use the technique with your child.

3. Set aside fifteen minutes a day to share time with your child.

4. Get your husband involved and/or interested in teaching the child.

5. Use positive reinforcement to teach the game Follow-the-Arrow.

6. Get together your teaching supplies—chalkboard, chalk, and eraser; start a Language Center; and make tactile letter cards.

7. Find a place to hold class and store your teaching materials in.

8. Designate a certain time each day, five days a week for class.

THREE

Thirty Days of Play

Some imaginative mothers have no trouble concocting creative things to do with a preschooler. A simple family outing can fire them up with enough energy, enthusiasm, and ideas to last for days. Why, these women can take their kids to the beach one week and have them constructing aquariums, discussing marine life, designing seashell collages, and talking like Jacques Cousteau the next week.

Of course when you're overworked, underpatienced, and secretly suspect your memory banks were cleared in the labor room along with your sinuses, you don't do all this. You just *feel* you should and perhaps this chapter can help.

This chapter contains thirty learning games for a month of play and relaxation between parent and child. Some of the games were developed by child-care experts and are used in nursery schools throughout the country. Others are the genius of resourceful mothers who wanted creative ways to survive captivity with a preschooler. Regardless of the origin, all these games have one thing in common. They are fun ways to spend quality time with your youngster. Here are some other points that make these games especially nice:

1. They are easy to make. You don't have to worry about power drills, socket wrenches, or complicated blueprints. As a matter of fact, if you've begun the Language Center (see Chapter Two), you have already made many of the materials.

2. Each of the games can be adjusted to suit your child's mental development, individual temperament, and attention span, and your patience.

3. They don't take much time. The average playing time is about ten or fifteen minutes—even less if your little angel likes to destroy things.

4. A few of the games can be played without adult supervision. (Of course you don't do this very often. But once in a while your telephone needs answering; your casserole needs stirring; and your other child, who's tap-dancing on the TV, needs stopping.)

5. Even though all the games can be played within a month, you and your child can enjoy them throughout his early years. And more than likely, you'll wear out the games quicker than your child's desire to play them.

Remember: the purpose of these games is to teach skills, but the focus of these games should be fun, so don't press the panic button if your little Johnny can't play all of these games or any of these games well. All kids can't do all things equally well or at the same age. (That's why they have mothers.) If your child has trouble with any game, skip it and try the game again a few months later.

Assignment #1. Play

Your first and only assignment for this chapter is to set aside a few minutes each day to laugh, grin, giggle, tickle, and play these games with your child. Imagine yourself Snow White in sneakers, Peter Pan in pantyhose, or even Bill Cosby without pudding, and begin Thirty Days of Play.

GAME 1   OUCHLESS OBSTACLE COURSE

So-called because Mom selects the equipment from among her softest furniture.

RELATED SKILLS
Body Awareness
Large Motor Development
Memory
Following Directions
Vocabulary

Arrange miscellaneous pieces of furniture in a jungle gym fashion so that your child can go from one piece to the next and develop a number of skills in the process. Start with simple directions such as crawl under the table, through the box, and jump over the pillow, and gradually add more furniture and more instructions as your child's skills increase. If you're really ambitious, include a walk-the-line exercise using chalk, paper, tape, or boards.

GAME 2   FOLLOW-THE-ARROW

Automatic left-to-right progression in reading is essential.

RELATED SKILLS
Left-to-Right Orientation
Tracking

Draw a long horizontal arrow in the middle of the chalkboard. Make sure the point faces the right end of the board. Take your finger and trace the arrow going from left to right. As you do, say, "The arrow goes this way." Ask your child to show you which way the arrow goes. Repeat the game on a plain sheet of paper and practice often until the child gets the point. You can even use miniature racing cars that "ride down" the arrow and show which way it goes.

Variation: Draw geometric figures above the arrow and ask your child to point to each object sitting on the arrow. Make sure he starts left and continues right. By the way, if you're having trouble teaching him left from right, here are two easy ways: 1. Show him his left hand and his right hand, now squeeze his right hand a few times each day and remind him that you're squeezing only his right hand. 2. Tape an R in his shoe or boot or write an R on his right hand.

GAME 3   TIN CAN ALLEY

Save up empty tin cans for this game and be sure there are no sharp edges.

RELATED SKILLS
Large Motor Development
Small Motor Development
Classifying
Language Development

Line up about three clean, empty tin cans of different sizes—small, medium, and large. Give your child a group of small, medium, and large-sized objects (such as balls) and ask him to drop the small objects in the small cans (tuna cans, cat food cans), the medium-sized objects into the medium-sized cans (16 oz. to 20 oz. fruit and vegetable cans), and the large objects into the large cans (32 oz. cans and larger). Gradually increase the line-up to include tiny and huge cans.

Commercial Educational Games

Incidentally, there are a lot of commercial educational games on the market and the general rule is that with a little creativity and time you can make your own at a fraction of the cost. But besides this economical point, there are a few other considerations. Many of these games are so profusely illustrated, cleverly packaged, and skillfully marketed that after sifting through numerous distractions you often discover your fancy toy is just a run-of-the-mill matching or sorting game all dressed up. This discovery is especially confusing to the child who, having faithfully memorized advertising slogans and cheerfully sung along to commercial jingles, expected this game to be no less than the second coming of Santa. He's apt to be so disappointed (or bored) that he may actually discard the toy and prefer to play with the ten-cent box it came in. Now don't misunderstand me, cardboard boxes make great toys, but it is a bit depressing to spend $7.95 just to find that out.

GAME 4   LOTTA-LOTTO

You'll get more mileage out of this game than almost any other. It's fun to play seated at a table or lying on the floor with a large piece of cardboard.

RELATED SKILLS
Language Development
Classifying
Small Motor Development

A simple game of picture lotto can be made by selecting a picture card and having your child find similar or identical pictures from a separate pile. For instance, select a picture of an apple and ask your child to go through the Language Center and find pictures of other fruit.

Variation: Alike and Different. After your child has completed a category of fruits, mammals, birds, or whatever, go through each category and talk about the qualities that make each member alike and each member different from the others. If he has a strawberry picture card and an apple picture card, you might say they are alike in that they are both fruit and both red, but they are different in how they look, taste, feel, and smell.

GAME 5   SOUND ZOO

This is fun to play while lying in bed together and helps prepare children for phonics reading.

RELATED SKILL
Auditory Discrimination

Collect some picture cards of animals and tell your child to pretend he's at a sound zoo where animals are identified by their sounds only, not their names. Hold up one picture at a time and ask him to give the sound that animal makes.

GAME 6   BISCUIT BAKE

This game will help your child better understand quantity.

RELATED SKILL
Logic

You'll need:
    A container of ready-to-bake biscuits
    Flour
Sprinkle two biscuits with a little flour. Let your child inspect the biscuits and ask him if they are the same size. When he agrees that they are the same size, roll one up into a ball. Ask him if the two biscuits would still taste the same and remain the same size after baking. Bake the biscuits and let the child eat them. While he is munching away, mention how the shape doesn't change the biscuits' size and taste.

GAME 7   STORYTIME

Children learn from example. And no matter how much lip service you give to the importance of reading, your child will pay no attention if your favorite book is the yellow pages. About the best place to get books for little or no cost is the public library. If you haven't been there recently you're in for a pleasant surprise. Gone are the staid librarians who once patrolled the corridors like SS guards and in their place are friendly, helpful people who like kids. Gone are those dreary grays and browns and in their place are bright yellows, sunset oranges, and golden tans.

Once you've taken this first crucial step and visited the public library with your child then relax around a warm fire, snuggle up on a fluffy bed or stretch out on a plush carpet and share the treasures you've brought home. Be sure to read stories to your child often and make Storytime an ongoing part of your at-home learning program.

GAME 8   RESTAURANT

RELATED SKILLS
Language Development
Classifying
Small Motor Development

Gather picture cards of many things that might be found at a restaurant and place them on a table. Include pictures of silverware, glasses, foods, napkins, serving dishes, pitchers of milk, etc. Ask your child to plan a meal he might eat at a restaurant. After he has arranged the place setting and selected a "meal" discuss the categories of food on each picture. Dairy products—yogurt, milk, cheese, etc. Vegetables—carrots, peas, potatoes, etc. Fruits— apples, oranges, bananas. Meats, eggs, and poultry. Cereals— bread, noodles, rice, breakfast cereals. Perhaps you could follow up this game by letting your child help plan and prepare a balanced meal for the family.

GAME 9   PICKPOCKET LADY

RELATED SKILLS
Classifying
Language Development

Put objects of varying textures in each pocket of an apron with several pockets, such as a chef's or carpenter's apron. One pocket might contain hard objects—rocks, marbles, silverware, etc.; another pocket might contain soft objects—cotton balls, sponges, yarn; and another pocket might contain rough objects—sandpaper, emery board. Ask your child to describe the objects in each pocket by the way they feel. After he has finished describing the object by "touch" alone, let him pick your pocket and see how accurate his description was. No apron? Put objects of varying textures inside a paper bag or box and ask your child to feel and describe the objects inside.

GAME 10   STRING ALONG

This activity is a standard in Montessori schools.

RELATED SKILLS
Small Motor Development
Seeing Patterns
Attention Span
Visual Discrimination

Stringing interesting objects can provide children with hours of happy, quiet play. Materials that work well include wooden and plastic beads, straight pieces of macaroni noodles, short pieces of cut drinking straws. Shoelaces, yarn, and plastic lacing make good cords.

Variation: Edible String-Along. If you don't mind the sugar, edible string-alongs can be made from string licorice and lifesavers. You might even get the other members of the family interested in this one.

GAME 11   FAMILY FOOT

You'll need:

Heavy wrapping or mailing paper
(The paper bags you get from the grocery store are good if you iron out the wrinkles.)
Magic Markers
Scissors

RELATED SKILLS
Comparing
Ordering

Get the members of your family to trace an outline of one another's feet—shoe and all. If your child can handle scissors, let him cut out the patterns. After each pattern has been cut out, write the identifying name on each. Line them up on the floor or on a table according to size. Ask questions about the size of each pattern such as, "Who has the biggest foot?" "Who has the smallest foot?" "Who has the next smallest foot?" You can tape these family feet over a fireplace, on the ceiling, or somewhere in the child's bedroom. When grandparents or favorite aunts and uncles visit, collect patterns of their feet too.

GAME 12   EGG CARTON SWITCH

RELATED SKILLS

Memory
Language Development

Place two or three objects in an egg carton or muffin tin (one in each cup) and ask your child to touch and name each object. Now ask him to close or cover his eyes. Remove one object. Have the child open his eyes and try to name the object that is missing. As your child becomes more proficient at playing "Egg Carton Switch" you can vary the game by: 1) removing more than one object at a time, 2) increasing the number of objects you put in, or 3) letting him be the teacher.

GAME 13   STACIA'S SYNONYM MATCH

Stacia's my niece and she and her mother play this vocabulary-building game all the time.

RELATED SKILL
Language Development

Think of a noun your child is familiar with and ask her to give you another name for it. If she can't supply a synonym, give her one. The game goes something like this: Ask, "Can you think of another word for *street*?" The child is silent. Prompt her by saying, "The car went down the *street* . . . The car went down the *road* . . . *Road* and *street* are synonyms and they mean the same or almost the same thing." Of course if you want to be big-headed about it you could say avenue, boulevard, thoroughfare, and so on.

Variation: After your child has had practice finding synonyms for nouns, try playing synonym match using adjectives.

GAME 14   LIDS AND BOTTLES

RELATED SKILLS
Small Motor Development
Attention Span
Visual Discrimination

Collect several different kinds of containers with lids: peanut butter jars, film containers, shampoo bottles, etc. Remove the tops and put them in a large bag or box. Ask the child to try to fit the lids on the proper containers. Start with about three or four containers and gradually build up your collection. (Make sure all containers are clean and free of sharp edges.)

GAME 15   CHALKBOARD JUNGLE

This game helps kids determine what is visually significant on a page.

RELATED SKILL
Reading

Draw a simple picture of an animal on the chalkboard and then draw several straight or wavy lines (top to bottom) over the picture. Ask your child to find the animal that is hiding in the jungle. Play this game a couple of times using different animals and gradually increase the number of lines you add. (See Figure 1.)

Figure 1

GAME 16   EMERGENCY

Think of several potentially dangerous situations and ask your child what he would do in each emergency.

RELATED SKILLS
Logic
Problem Solving

Example: You go to turn on the television and a spark jumps out. What do you do?

Example: Your ball rolls in the street, you want to get it, but a car is coming—what do you do?

Disagreeing on an Emergency

The only problem with this practical game is that you and your child may disagree on the basic premise of what is and what is not an emergency. Your idea of an emergency is a grease fire, a car that won't start, a kid with a 104-degree temperature, and a mouse in the house. His idea of an emergency is bubble gum that won't blow, a misplaced rock, or an empty toilet tissue spindle. However, once that common ground is found, those of us who panic easily can take comfort knowing that in an emergency someone else can take charge.

GAME 17   PICTURE TALK

RELATED SKILLS
Reading
Language Development

Select several pictures of people at work, at play, in grocery stores, etc. from your Language Center. Ask the child what he sees and to tell you about what's happening in each picture. For instance, if the people are carrying umbrellas, ask your child what the weather is like. If the girl in the picture has a book bag, ask your child where she might be going. The idea is not only to get your child to describe the obvious, but to draw inferences which are not obvious from information that is there.

GAME 18   I'M THE BOSS

This game is quite enjoyable, especially when your child is familiar enough with it to reverse roles.

RELATED SKILLS
Following Directions
Memory
Large and Small Motor Development

Start the game by telling your child that you want him to do two things and for him to remember what to do and what order to do them in. For example, "Benjamin, turn on a light and bring me a book." If he can easily follow two directions, increase the number of directions to three and then to four. Example, "Turn off the light, pick up the pillow, and sit on the sofa."
Variation: Role Reversal. After your child has become familiar with the game "I'm the Boss," let him be the boss and give you instructions. You can encourage your child to give precise directions by responding to his directions with the broadest possible interpretation. For instance if he says, "Go to the door and shut it," get down on all fours, crawl to the door, shut it and remain there until he gives you directions to come back.

GAME 19   RHYME-TIME

RELATED SKILLS
Language Development
Auditory Discrimination

Locate a series of rhyming pictures in your Language Center such as can, man, pan, fan, or pop, top, mop, etc. Put each rhyming set into a separate envelope and paste one picture from the set on front of the envelope. Now enclose a picture that does not rhyme. Make about three or four sets and encourage your child to find the rhyming words in each envelope. If your child has had little or no rhyming experience he may find this game too difficult. You can provide additional rhyming experiences through nursery rhymes, read-aloud children's poetry, and spontaneous rhyme play. A children's librarian could recommend rhyming stories your child might enjoy.

Why Learning Colors Is Important

Some kids pick up the concept of color easily and on their own. Others don't. But how your child learns color is not as important as that he learn it because identifying objects by color is one of the first steps toward classifying similar objects.

GAME 20   COLOR CODED

RELATED SKILLS
Classification
Language Development

Cut two sets of 2 in. by 4 in. colored paper or cardboard rectangles (about the size of playing cards). Start with red, blue, yellow, black, and white. Give one set to your child and keep one set for yourself. Hold up one of your cards and explain: "This card is red. Now find your red card." When the child finds the red card, ask him to tell you its color. Give him a kiss or hug for selecting the correct one. If he has no concept of color names you might go over red, blue, and yellow in the first session. Gradually introduce white, black, green, orange, purple, and tan.

Variation: Mix up the cards and have the child find the matching pair.

By the way, if your child has trouble learning red (confusing it with green and brown), don't immediately assume he's color blind. He may be too young to learn colors. Give him a couple of months and try it again later.

GAME 21 ANN'S ANTONYM MATCH GAME

This is essentially the reverse of the synonym game.

RELATED SKILL
Language Development

Tell your child you are going to play a game where you give him one word and he has to think of another word that is very different from or the opposite of that word. Start the game by using examples of opposites in the context of a sentence such as, "Don't turn the water *on,* turn it *off.*" "If you jump *up,* you'll come *down.*" Later as your child understands the words "opposite" and "antonym," you'll be able to just give him a word and ask him to supply the opposite word. Some common antonyms are listed below:

long-short	rough-smooth
big-little	wet-dry
hot-cold	wide-narrow
happy-sad	sick-well
fast-slow	on-off
day-night	over-under
same-different	clean-dirty
dark-light	fat-skinny
old-new	young-old
good-bad	open-close
up-down	hard-soft
boy-girl	full-empty

GAME 22   WORD PAINTING

The idea here is to "paint" a noun by using an adjective to describe it.

RELATED SKILL
Language Development

Gather up about five or six of the child's favorite toys. Hold up one toy at a time and ask him, "What is this?" If he says "Ball," respond "Blue ball," "Beach ball," "Rubber ball," or "Tennis ball." The point is to extend the child's language and encourage him to be more specific about the unique qualities of each object.
Variation: After you've played this game many times with real objects, try playing it with words. Tell the child you're going to paint the word "girl" and rattle off two or three adjectives to describe girl such as happy girl, pretty girl, quiet girl, etc. Ask your child to do likewise.

GAME 23   PAINLESS PUZZLES

These homemade puzzles are painless for two reasons. For parents they're painless because they don't cost much. For kids they are painless because the level of difficulty and frustration is controlled by the parent.

RELATED SKILLS
Small Motor Development
Perceptual Development
Attention Span

Select large (5 in. by 7 in. pictures or bigger) pictures of animals, people, furniture, plants, etc. from your Language Center. Paste a piece of cardboard onto the back and then cut the picture in half, thirds, quarters, or in a random design. Store the puzzle in an envelope and enclose (on a separate sheet) a scale outline of the completed puzzle along with the pieces. Give the pieces to your child and ask him to complete the puzzle. He can use your outline as a reference.

GAME 24   PREPOSITION POSITION

RELATED SKILLS
Spatial Relationship
Language Development

Find a shoebox with a lid on top and one of your child's favorite small toy animals. Tell your child you are going to put the toy animal *on* the box. After you demonstrate, give the box and the toy to your child and ask him to put the toy *on* the box. When he does you should clap, shout, smile, and act very pleased. Continue with about one or two prepositions and gradually include others. Be sure to transfer the use of prepositions into your everyday language with the child, e.g., "Find the ball underneath the sofa," "Sit beside me," "Walk around the table," etc. Some common prepositions are listed below:

in, on, near, far from, behind, in front of, over, under, on top of, inside, around, in the corner, on the edge, in the middle of

One way to liven up this game is to animate the animals as they demonstrate the various positions. Make the horses gallop around the box, the frogs croak over the box, the birds chirp near the box, etc. Remember to let your child be teacher once in a while.

GAME 25   TONGUE TWISTER

This will help limber up your child's tongue for phonics work later.

You'll need:
Peanut Butter
Spoon
Honey

1. Put a dab of peanut butter behind the child's upper front teeth and ask him to lick it off. Now put a dab behind the lower front teeth and ask him to lick it off.
2. Ask your child to stick his tongue out as far as he can. Ask him to do it again and this time drop a little honey on the tip of his tongue.
3. Ask your child if he can touch his tongue to his chin. Ask if he can touch his tongue to his nose.
4. Encircle the outside of his lips with a thin coating of honey. Ask him to lick off the honey by circling his tongue clockwise or counterclockwise.

GAME 26   ONE BOX, TWO BOX

This game is designed to help your child look for and classify objects with similar qualities or attributes.

RELATED SKILLS
Classifying
Language Development

You'll need:
    Two large cardboard boxes
    Your child's toys

Tell your child that you and he are going to put his toys into two groups or sets. All the hard toys are to go into one box (toy cars, wooden blocks, toy guns, models, etc.) and all the soft toys are to go into another box (stuffed animals, puppets, doll clothes, rubber balls, etc.). After your child has played the game one or two times and learned the difference between hard and soft and which group (set) each toy belongs to, you can vary the game and re-sort the toys based upon another similar attribute. For instance, you could re-sort the toys based upon weight (heavy toys–light toys); size (big toys–little toys); and personal preference (toys I like and toys I don't like).

Variation 1: Encourage your child to develop his own sorting system. For instance the clean toys would go in one box and the dirty toys might go in another box.

Variation 2: To find similarities and differences within a group or set take one group of toys, such as the hard toys, and re-sort them into two different groups. For example, the hard toys with wheels would go in one box, while the hard toys without wheels would go in another box. This game can get quite complicated so be sure to talk about only one or two attributes at a time.

GAME 27   TASTE TEST

RELATED SKILLS
Language
Classifying

Put samples of foods that have similar tastes in small containers such as cups or bowls. Encourage your child to sample at least one food from each group, but don't insist on it.[1] Examples of foods with similar tastes include: Salty— anchovies, table salt, baking soda. Sweet—bits of fruit, honey, sugar. Sour—vinegar, pickle, lemon slices. Bitter—cream of tartar, basil leaves. (This group tastes horrible so consider either taste-testing very tiny amounts or eliminating this group altogether.) As your child samples foods within a similar taste group, talk about how foods can be grouped by taste: "These are all salty," "This group is sweet," etc. In your discussion be sure to mention that "Taste Test" is a game to play only with Mama and that taste-testing foods on his own can be very dangerous.

Puppet Play

Finally, you can brighten up almost any dull afternoon with a little puppet play. A number of good books on making and using puppets are available at most public libraries and here are a few

---

1. As we already know, some children won't eat anything that wasn't conceived under a golden arch, so don't make it a big deal if your child refuses to co-operate.

easy-to-manipulate puppets you can make with a minimum of materials. Of course if you're exceptionally energetic you could add a theater, sew costumes, pop popcorn, and make the project a family affair.

GAME 28   FINGER PUPPETS

RELATED SKILLS
Reading
Language Development

A simple finger puppet can be made by using a magic marker to draw a face on your (or your child's) favorite finger. To give your puppet "clothes" simply poke a hole in a kleenex or napkin and slide it over your finger. If you are handy with knitting needles you might consider knitting a wardrobe of jackets, hats, skirts, etc., for your finger puppet.

Another simple finger puppet can be made by affixing an animal or human face to a ring or paper tube and sliding it over the tip of your finger. (See Figure 2.)

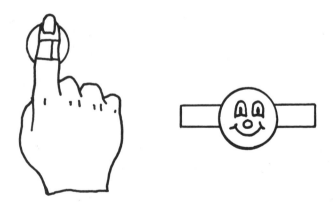

Figure 2

GAME 29   POPSICLE STICK PUPPET

RELATED SKILLS
Reading
Language Development

Rod puppets are especially good for young children who may lack the dexterity to manipulate their fingers and hands skillfully. To make a simple rod puppet merely glue a cut-out picture onto a popsicle stick, tongue depressor, or wooden spoon. Be sure to leave enough room at the bottom of the stick for a handle. (See Figure 3.) To animate your puppet move it up and down, in and out, or spin it around.

Figure 3

GAME 30   SOCK PUPPET

RELATED SKILLS
Reading
Language Development

An old sock offers endless adaptations as a puppet. Buttons can be eyes; yarn can become hair, eyebrows, and fringes; pipe cleaners can be antennas, mustaches, etc. (See Figure 4.)

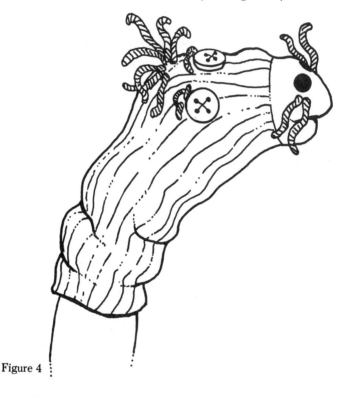

Figure 4

Overdoing Games

The way I see things, kids can stand almost anything except boredom. And one of the quickest ways to bore a child is to play a game that is no fun or overdo a game that was fun. Games that are no fun are not really a problem; you can't even bribe kids to play them. It's overdoing the fun games that causes problems and puts you and your child on a collision course. And usually this family feud starts so innocently.

You find a game you love, the child loves; in fact, the whole family loves it. But instead of varying the game and changing it up a bit, you get hooked. You find yourself playing the same game in the car, at the park, in between meals, and right before bedtime. One mother confessed to waking her kids up early on Saturdays just to get the excitement going.

Then without warning, things begin to slip a little. The game that was once as clean and crisp as a new dollar bill takes on the appearance of wilted lettuce. Pieces start mysteriously disappearing. The child who once bubbled with excitement and enthusiasm would rather count leaves in the wallpaper than play along. He may pretend not to notice if you cheat! Finally the kid gets fed up, and he props a warm teddy bear beside you, bequeaths you the game in his will, and then disappears.

This nasty episode could have been avoided by simply taking a few precautionary steps. First, don't play the game over and over until it is as exciting as last year's Play-Doh. Use the variations and don't be afraid to invent new games of your own. Second, change your Language Center materials frequently and update your games to keep them challenging and interesting. If you've exhausted your own supply of pictures start asking friends for theirs. Better yet, find another parent to swap and trade ideas with.

After all, playing these games is secondary to you and your child's enjoying each other's company.

SUMMARY OF ASSIGNMENTS FOR CHAPTER THREE

Play the games in this chapter with your child.

FOUR
Open Sesame

The fact that many mothers are teaching their preschoolers to read is perhaps the best-kept secret since Miss Clairol asked, "Does she or doesn't she?" Apparently while the experts debate the value of early reading instruction many average, ordinary, brownie-baking mothers have taken matters into their own hands and are successfully and privately teaching their children how to read at home.

And with a little training, so can you.

I know all about the gloomy opposition: educators who consider reading instruction their private domain, horror stories about bright and bored kids who throw spit balls behind teachers' backs, and intimidating case histories about two-year-olds who taught themselves how to read by watching R-O-L-A-I-D commercials; but I'm not convinced mothers can't and shouldn't teach reading, and neither are the thousands of women who do teach and who have found it one of the most gratifying and delightful experiences of parenthood. One mother of six said of her decision to teach:

> . . . My first child was ready to read in 1955
> and I made the decision at that point that I was
> not going to let him be ruined by the schools

and that I was going to teach him to read at home by the phonics method so that he would have the essential tool to all learning—which is the ability to read. So I did that, and then entered him in second grade and did the same with all my other children and they all think that's the most important thing I gave them because you really can't be an achiever and do well in school unless you can read. . . .

Phyllis Schlafly, 1981

Many researchers in the field of early childhood education confirm our feelings about the virtues of at-home reading instruction. Their findings have shown:

1. children who read before the first grade are likely to retain a lead over children who don't for at least the next five years of schooling, and with continuing accelerated instruction, that lead can last indefinitely;

2. learning to read at an early age develops a pattern for success that transfers over into other areas such as math and science;

3. parents who teach their own children strengthen the bond of communication and respect between parent and child and lessen the probability of discipline and social problems later;

4. young children make little distinction between work and play and to them learning to read is another way to have fun with their parents.

Now, all things considered, don't the rewards of becoming an active participant in your child's education outweigh the possibility of ruffling a few academic feathers?

APPROACHES TO READING

Because the educational community is split on precisely which approach to reading is best, concerned parents have had to venture out alone and develop their own method of reading instruction. Consequently, at-home reading programs have varied from the practical approach which teaches a rudimentary vocabulary such as "hot" and "cold," to the prodigious approach which teaches words like "erudite" and "piquant" and prepares tots for the California Bar Exam. Yet interestingly enough, research indicates that despite the wide variances in approaches, when parents teach, the majority of the children learn to read.

Of course that doesn't mean teaching reading is as easy as pie, and for those of you who lack the time or prior teaching experience to develop your own program, or who harbor fears of "messing up," or who still smart from the rigors of toilet training, there is a simple and effective approach to beginning reading that has been used successfully by novices and professionals alike. That approach is a combination of phonics instruction and a limited sight-word vocabulary.

Phonics is a sensible, logical method of teaching children to read that associates a spoken sound with a printed letter symbol. Instead of talking about a letter's name, we talk about the sound it makes, either alone or in combination with other letters. The main strength of phonics lies in its simplicity and transfer value. Once a child has mastered the symbols for decoding and a few basic rules, he can use that knowledge to read up to 87 percent of the words he comes across.

A phonics approach to reading works especially well with young children because its emphasis on sound duplication and word patterns takes advantage of newly acquired language skills and children learn how to read in much the same way they learned how to talk.[1]

Phonics is effective with older children having problems learning to read because the simple step-by-step, sound-by-

1. Knowledge of the names of the letters is not necessary for beginning reading instruction. However, teaching the letter names will be covered in Chapter Seven.

sound approach allows for immediate feedback and helps prevent reading problems from accumulating over a long period of time. And with phonics, reading instruction begins immediately and without the delay of reading-readiness programs, standardized tests, and word lists.

Even though phonics is effective as a tool to get kids started reading, it does have a few shortcomings: not all words in our language sound out or follow simple linguistic rules, and because other languages have affected English, there are many unexpected spellings. Those words which follow no easily decodable pattern are best taught as "sight words" and must be learned by memorization.

The use of sight words as an approach to reading instruction is probably most familiar to those of us who were products of the post-World War II baby boom. We learned to read our Dick and Jane books by memorization or by the look-and-say method and sometimes that meant spending a full year being drilled (or should I say being grilled?) over the same 200 to 300 words.

However, when phonics is used in combination with a limited sight word vocabulary, the time devoted to sheer memorization is reduced substantially and a child who would ordinarily spend a year memorizing a few hundred words is now able to read thousands of words and dozens of library books in the same amount of time.

The inherent advantage for your child is that he will not only easily read "See Spot Run" but he'll be able to read classics such as *Peter Pan* and *Treasure Island* while he's still young enough to enjoy and appreciate them.

READING F U N DAMENTALS

To help make your child's introduction to reading a fun, exciting experience I've included a reading comic strip based on two wacky cartoon characters—Daisy, the hippopotamus, and Macadoo, the bird. The Dr. Seuss stories, the *Sesame Street* characters, and much else have already demonstrated how humor can capture a child's attention and imagination, and keeping in that fun tradition, Daisy and Macadoo introduce a series of reading lessons that amuse as well as teach children how to read.

Step-by-step instructions for the first twenty-six lessons to go with the reading comic strip are included later in this chapter, but before you plunge ahead into the reading lessons I suggest you first set aside a week to complete the next three prereading assignments.

These assignments can be played as games on car trips, during waits at the doctor's office, or with other members of the family helping. The idea is to mix fun and learning and make the most of the time you and your child have together.

Some of these assignments are variations of exercises used in the highly effective DISTAR and Montessori programs and others are variations of games commonly played by parents and children. However, all of these preliminary exercises introduce a series of sub-skills which help make your child's transition from non-reader to reader smoother, easier, and more likely.

Assignment #1. Rhyme

Rhyme is a valuable skill because it helps your child understand the relationship between words having similar endings and provides him with a tool that makes easier sounding out phonetically similar words. In the course of free-play, parent and child often develop their own rhyming games and your first assignment for this chapter is to play rhyming games with your child for the next week. You can either play a favorite rhyming game of your own or the one described below called "Rhyme-It." Here's how it goes:

Mother: "Listen, I am going to rhyme with . . . *it*. What word am I going to rhyme with?"

Child: "It."

Mother: "Sssiiit, fffiiit, mmmiiit, rhyme with . . . *it*. Can you give me a word that rhymes with . . . *it*?"

Correct responses are any word (including the ones you gave) or any nonsense word that rhymes with . . . *it*. You can, of course, substitute any word for *it* and if your child has difficulty rhyming, either prompt, or lead him by way of example, or give him the answer. By the way, this game can be played almost anytime or anywhere and one fringe benefit is that the next time your little angel decides to play "Get Mama" or "Wreck the Joint" you'll have on-hand a quick diversionary tactic.

Assignment #2. Listening Games

It's a funny thing about a child's ears. The same ears that can't hear "Clean up your room" at two paces can tune in on private conversations held behind closed doors. As your child's teacher you'll of course want to direct his acuity toward more scholarly endeavors and the next two listening games show you how. These games prepare your child for phonics reading because they help him break words down into their component sounds and they encourage practice blending sounds into words. (Unfortunately, they don't do a thing for terminal nosiness!)

1. Slow Poke

In the game Slow Poke the mother says a word very slowly and the child translates the slow poke word into a word spoken at a normal rate (says it fast). Here's how it works:

Mother: "Let's play the game Slow Poke. I'm going to say a word slowly and I want you to tell me what word I'm saying. Here goes . . . uuuuup."
Child: "Up."
Mother: "Rrrrrraaaaat."
Child: "Rat."
Mother: "Sssssseeee."
Child: "See."

This game is easier than it may seem and if you 1) begin with one syllable words, 2) limit your sessions to about eight or ten words, and 3) praise enthusiastically after correct answers, the activity is more funlike than worklike.

2. Word Division

Word Division helps a child identify when a change in sound occurs within each word. Say a word slowly (as in Slow Poke) and have your child clap each time he hears a different sound.

Example A   Dividing the word RUG

clap   clap

rrr   uuu ↑ g ↑

Example B   Dividing the word SAND

clap   clap   clap

sss aaa ↑ nnn ↑ d ↑

For now, keep the sessions brief and stick to one syllable words. Young children often have trouble recognizing sound changes so don't worry if your child can't identify every change in sound within a word. However, if after several practice sessions your child fails to pick up any changes in sounds, and you're certain he doesn't have a hearing problem, he may need more practice developing his auditory discrimination skills. For now skip Word Division and play some of the other listening games he enjoys in Chapter Three. The listening games in Chapter Three include: Game 5 (Sound Zoo), Game 18 (I'm the Boss), and Game 19 (Rhyme-Time). After he's had more practice with other listening games, try playing Word Division again. Assignment #2 is to practice the listening games Slow Poke and Word Division a few minutes each day for the next week.

Assignment #3. Follow-the-Arrow

There is a lot of confusion about what dyslexia is and isn't. Consequently, many parents are needlessly suffering anxiety attacks when little Sara writes TAC rather than CAT. New research suggests that dyslexia originates in the brain and interferes with a child's ability to acquire speech, reading, or other cognitive skills. Young children with dyslexia may have: inability to recognize rhymes, difficulty remembering or reading words, trouble following directions, or unusual difficulties with spelling or writing assignments.

Research from Yale University suggests that children with dyslexia are not more prone to reversing letters or words than the general population. But children who learn to read solely by the whole language or sight word approach may tend to reverse letters. Sometimes, these children are mislabeled "dyslexic." You can help prevent your child from having problems reversing letters by teaching him to read with phonics and playing games such as *Slow Poke, Word Division,* and *Follow the Arrow.*

TEACHING READING

You and your child are now about to begin what may well be the most important journey of his life—learning to read. As adults we take this miraculous ability for granted, but to a child the world of reading is a strange place of funny-looking squiggly lines and further evidence of his own powerlessness.

By teaching a child to read you contribute to his knowledge and independence as well as grant him a measure of control in an unpredictable, often confusing world.

Are you ready?

This role calls for your most consummate and compassionate performance yet and the remainder of this chapter is your script.

The Basics

The teaching format presented is essentially a six-step procedure. The basic points are summarized here:

1. Assemble your teaching materials.
2. Review old sounds.
3. Use the chalkboard and tactile letter cards to introduce the new sound.

4. Practice words that contain the new sound—orally, on the chalkboard, and with Language Center pictures.
5. Read the comic strip to your child.
6. Play reading games based on the new sound.

This six-step format is standard (except for a few variations) for each reading lesson and it's a good idea to learn the basic format first, and then modify it to suit your individual teaching style and available time.

The Procedure

To get a more specific idea of what to teach, when to teach it, and how to teach it, let's mentally run through a detailed example of Reading Lesson 1.

Reading Lesson 1—Teaching "m"

STEP 1. Gather your *materials*: the chalkboard, chalk, tactile letter cards, Language Center pictures, the reading comic strips, and materials for the reading activity. Be prepared to make your child the focus of your love, attention, and affection.

STEP 2. *Review* old sounds. Use the tactile letter cards to review the sounds that have already been taught. Go in a flash card sequence. (Since "m" is the first lesson there are no previous sounds. Omit this step for Lesson 1.)

STEP 3a. Write the upper-case and lower-case letter for the new sound on the *chalkboard*. Point to the letters and say, "These letters make the m-m-m sound." Ask child, "What sound do these letters make?" The child answers, "M-m-m." At this point you should be and act very happy, excited, and pleased. Your child has attached a spoken sound to a printed symbol and taken the first step toward literacy, and the magnitude of this accomplishment is no less significant than his first wobbly step. Now express your joy and give your remarkable child the biggest hug and kiss you can.

STEP 3b. Hold up the "m" *sandpaper letter* and say, "This letter makes the m-m-m sound. What sound does this letter make?"

Again, you should hug, praise, and say something like, "Because you can tell me what sound this letter makes, I'm going to let you touch it." Give the letter to your child and direct his finger across its surface as though he were writing with his finger. As you do this, point out the letter's unique configuration—humps, tail, curve, or whatever.

STEP 4a. *Oral Practice.* Select about three to five words from the "Oral Practice Word List" in Lesson 1. Ask your child to listen for the "m" sound in each word and to repeat each word after you.

STEP 4b. Locate *pictures* in the Language Center which begin with the "m" sound and share these pictures with your child. You could introduce the pictures by saying something like, "Let's talk about some things that begin with 'm-m-m.'"

STEP 4c. *On Board Practice.*
Refer to the "On Board Practice Word List." Select a word from the list and help your child blend the sounds into a word. Select a few more words and help your child read them. (This step is omitted for Lessons 1–10 because your child won't learn how to read words until Lesson 11.)

STEP 5.   Read the *comic strip* to your child.

STEP 6.   *Reading Activity.* Refer to the "Reading Activity" section of Lesson 1 and play the game with your child.

The Plan

Here is a lesson plan format that summarizes the preceding information and provides guidelines on how to organize each lesson.

LESSON PLAN CHECKLIST

Sounds Taught _____ Lesson # _____ Date _____
Sounds Reviewed _____ New Sound _____
Material Needed
Chalkboard and Chalk _____ Tactile Letter Cards _____
Pictures from Language Center _____ Comic Strip _____
Materials prepared for reading activity _____
Check Steps Completed
1. Materials assembled _____
2. Old sounds reviewed _____
3. New sound introduced
   On Board _____
   Tactile Letter Cards _____
4. Word Practice
   Orally ____ Language Center Pictures ____ On Board _____
5. Comic Strip
   Read by parent _____ Read by child _____
6. Completed Activity _____

Assignment #4. Open Sesame

As your child's teacher, it's your turn to nudge and instruct your little fledging on his maiden voyage into the world of literature and literacy. Your fourth assignment for this chapter is to complete Lessons 1 through 29 with your child and teach him how to read. Follow the six-step format for the first couple of lessons to get a feel for what you're doing, and then modify the teaching format to suit your needs.

Remember to teach these letters as the sounds, not as the names of the alphabet. If you aren't familiar with the basic sounds of the alphabet you'll need to refer to the Reading Lesson Section and practice making the twenty-six sounds in isolation before you introduce them to your child.

Now look over the Lesson Plan Check List one more time, and then start teaching!

THE READING LESSON SECTION

Pacing

I'm told some precocious children can learn several sounds per day, but most children need to work on a sound at least one or two days before it's firmly fixed in their minds. Unless you're certain your little tyke is a budding genius, a rule of thumb is to introduce one sound per day, and don't hesitate to slow down or speed up introducing new sounds depending upon your child's rate of learning.

Learning how to read is not a cram course or a horse race, but a painstaking, deliberate process in which accuracy takes precedence over speed. Try to avoid making comparisons between children, and remember, while that freckled kid down the block may already be reading, your child is reaping the immeasurable benefits of being taught by a loving and supportive parent.

Besides, if your child is not yet in first grade he still has a few years before he'll be expected to read, so you can afford to take your time and concentrate on mastery.

And if your child is already in school and having trouble learning to read, he's already under enough pressure to perform. At this point in his education he needs to achieve a string of successes in a loving and relaxed atmosphere, and you can best help by not insisting on too rapid a learning pace.

LESSON 1   *m*

is the taste good sound, m-m-m. Before you introduce the sound to your child, practice saying it aloud in the words *mass* and *rim*. "M" is a continuous sound and try to keep the sound as pure as possible by not adding vowel sounds such as mi, me, mu, or mo. Its unique configuration is that it has two humps.

1. "M" Words for Further Practice.
    A. Oral Practice
        man, mat, milk, mad, me, mother
2. Reading Activity for the "M" Sound—Drinking Milk.

    Have a glass of plain or flavored milk with your child. As you drink the milk say m-m-m and encourage your child to do likewise.

LESSON 2   *t*

is the ticking of the clock sound, t-t-t. It is not continuous, and you say the sound only once. To hear the "t" sound, say the word *hit* aloud. Now say *tent*. Practice saying the sound to yourself a few times before you teach your child.

1. "T" Words for Further Practice.
    A. Oral Practice
        top, toy, tag, ten, tent, teeth

2. Reading Activity for the "T" Sound—Ticking Clock.

Let your child listen to the ticking of a wind-up clock or watch.

LESSON 3   s

is the hissing sound of snakes or of air being expelled from a tire. To hear a pure "s" sound, say the word *kiss*, now say *sip*. This sound is continuous and can be held s-s-s. ("S" can also sound like "z," as in "has," and you'll teach this sound as it occurs later on.)

1. "S" Words for Further Practice.
   A. Oral Practice
      sit, sam, sun, stop, sat, six
2. Reading Activity for the "S" Sound—Finger Puppets.

Make two snake finger puppets—one for you and one for your child. Pretend your fingers are snakes and make the s-s-s sound. (See Chapter Three, Game 28, for instructions on making finger puppets.)

Corrections

Any correction you make should be positive and painless. Remember the first time a teacher rapped you on the knuckles for not knowing the correct answer? Ouch. You too must refrain from using negative punishment or psychologically rapping your student on the knuckles with remarks such as, "That's wrong," or "You're not trying." When your child lacks the correct answer—give it to him or her—IMMEDIATELY!!! Your child wants to please you, immensely so, and you can give him or her every opportunity to do just that by not letting him flounder (wildly guessing or silently sweating out an answer) and by keeping corrections simple, brief, and non-punitive.

LESSON 4   b

is one of the first sounds babies make and some people say the "b" sound is the sound of milk being poured from a bottle. To hear the "b" sound say the words *cab* and *rib*. The "b" sound is difficult to pronounce completely free of additional vowel sounds, so you'll need to practice keeping it as pure as possible. Another problem area is that "b" is often confused with "d" or "p." To clear up some of the confusion about the similarity in shape you may want to write the "b" stem a bit shorter than the "d" stem.

1. "B" Words for Further Practice.
   A. Oral Practice
      bed, ball, boy, bubble, bam, bite
2. Reading Activity for the "B" Sound—Newspaper Sounds.

Give your child an old newspaper and a magic marker and have him circle all the "b"s he can find.

LESSON 5   r

is the sound of the roaring lion. It is continuous, and to hear the "r" sound, say the word *rug*. Now slowly say *rip*. Young children frequently mispronounce the "r" sound, and so do many adults. Some of the more common mispronunciations include er, are, and rer.

1. "R" Words for Further Practice.
   A. Oral Practice
      rat, run, rock, rip, rabbit, red
2. Reading Activity for the "R" Sound—Finger Tracing.

Pour a thin layer of Cream of Wheat onto a cookie sheet. Show your child how to trace the letter "r" in the Cream of

Wheat with his finger. Erase the "r" by gently shaking the cookie sheet.[2]

LESSON 6   *c*

is the coughing sound. To hear the "c" sound say the words *cat* and *picnic* aloud. "C" is not continuous and the sound is said only once. A few other sounds that make the "c" sound are k and ck. ("C" also makes a soft sound as in *nice*, but we'll talk about that later.)

1. "C" Words for Further Practice.
   A. Oral Practice
      cup, cat, can, cut, clip, cow
2. Reading Activity for the "C" Sound—Treasure Hunt.

   Write "c" on pieces of paper and hide them around the house. Encourage your child to find them and read the sounds.

LESSON 7   *g*

is the gulping sound. You can feel your throat move when you say it. Some say this is the sound frogs make. To hear the "g" sound, say the words *leg* and *rug*. "G" is written and printed differently, so your child may not be able to recognize "g" in all print types yet. ("G" also makes a soft sound as in *giant*, but we'll talk about the soft sound of "g" later.)

1. "G" Words for Further Practice.
   A. Oral Practice
      gum, goat, gate, gold, game, good, girl
2. Reading Activity for the "G" Sound—Finger Puppets.

2. This idea came from Marilyn Kay, director of the Reading Group, Urbana, Illinois.

Make two frog finger puppets—one for you and one for your child. Pretend they are frogs and make the "g" sound.

LESSON 8   *h*

is the sound you make when you run and get tired, h-h-h. It's especially hard to blend because it's not voiced[3] or continuous. When you teach the "h" sound, try not to add vowel sounds and you'll avoid blending problems later. To hear the "h" sound say the words *hit* and *hat*.

1. "H" Words for Further Practice.
   A. Oral Practice
      hat, hop, hill, help, hot, house
2. Reading Activity for the "H" Sound—Hug My Mug.

Have your child jog around the room and make the h-h-h sound. When he returns to you say, "I forgot to mention one more word that begins with the 'h' sound—hug!" Now give your child a big hug.

LESSON 9   *a*

is a vowel and you can tell your child that vowels are the strongest letters in the alphabet because every word must contain at least one vowel. Also, vowels sometimes say their names. To hear the sound "a" makes most of the time say the words *apple* and *ax*. Because "a" is written and printed differently, your child may not be able to identify "a" in various print types. The sound of "a" is continuous.

1. "A" Words for Further Practice.
   A. Oral Practice

3. The vocal cords do not vibrate.

apple, add, at, ax, am, ask
2. Reading Activity for the "A" Sound—Letter Necklace.

Write "a" on a small piece of cardboard and string it on a piece of yarn or shoelace. Let your child wear the letter necklace and ask him a few times throughout the day what sound the letter makes.

LESSON 10   v

is the sound of an airplane or a vacuum cleaner. It is continuous and to hear the "v" sound say the word *vase*. Now say *have* and hold the v-v-v. It's common for children to say b-b-b instead of v-v-v, so when you introduce the sound to your child be sure to get the full effect of the vibrations and put your teeth over your bottom lip.

1. "V" Words for Further Practice.
   A. Oral Practice
      vase, van, very, visit
2. Reading Activity for the "V" Sound—Airplane.

Fold a sheet of paper into an airplane or jet. Fly your airplane and when it is "airborne" encourage your child to supply the sound effects and make the v-v-v sound.

LESSON 11

Putting sounds together to form words is one of the most exciting and rewarding steps in learning to read. It's that moment of serendipity when the pieces of the puzzle fit together to make the whole and the sensation is as exhilarating as making the four corners in Bingo or pinpointing the who-dunnit in an Agatha Christie mystery. And now that your child knows several consonant sounds and one vowel sound he can crack the reading code and learn how to put the sounds together to make words.

To help your child blend sounds into words you'll need the chalkboard and a piece of chalk. (See Figure 5.)

1. Draw a large horizontal arrow on the chalkboard.

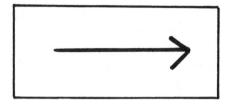

2. Draw the letter *a* on top of the arrow.

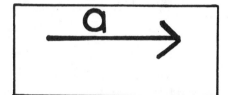

3. Point to the "a" and ask your child what sound the letter makes. (Child says "a-a-a.")

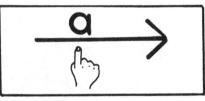

4. Now add *t* to make the word *at*.

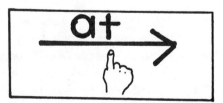

Figure 5

5. Ask your child to say each sound you touch and to listen for the word the sounds make.

6. Point to "a." (Child says "a-a-a.") Slide finger over to "t." (Child says "t.")

7. Go back and underscore the letters with your finger as you slowly say, "Aaat."

8. Ask your child what the word is. If he says "at," hug, kiss, and act very pleased. If he doesn't say "at," give him the answer and say "at."

9. Practice blending the word "at" a few more times. Encourage your child to read "at" by himself and blend the sounds into words.

10. Practice blending a few other words into sounds.

(What you are essentially doing is combining the previously played games "Slow Poke" and "Follow-the-Arrow.")

If your child has problems blending, and either adds extra sounds (e.g., says a-a-a-s-s-t instead of a-a-a-t) or takes gulps of air between sounds (e.g., a-a-a-breath-t), here are a few tricks to help:

Hold a miniature toy car beneath the beginning sound of the word. Move the car slowly from left to right and have the child say each sound the car "rides" under.

Another trick is to *gently* pinch the child's nose as he moves from one sound to the next. This pinch prevents him from taking gulps of air between sounds and for most children one or two pinches is plenty enough to get the idea.

Here are some words to practice on the chalkboard with your child:

rag	at	am	cab
tag	hat	ham	tab
bag	bat	bam	
sag	cat	Sam	
	rat		
	mat		
	sat		

Work on blending sounds into words for a couple of days before proceeding on to new lessons. Feel free to include rhyming words, nonsense words, or other letter combinations of your own.

Reading Activity—Making Reading Wheels

Reading Wheels are designed to help your child quickly review a number of different letter combinations. After your child has practiced blending several words into sounds on the board, make a Reading Wheel for him. Here's how:

Join two cardboard circles, one larger than the other, with a screw and nut or paper fastener. Write "a" on the outer edge of the smaller circle and write "m," "t," "b," "c," "v," on the edge of the larger wheel. Show your child how to turn the wheels to make words. See Figure 6.

Figure 6

You can get a lot of teaching mileage out of these Reading Wheels if you add additional vowels to the smaller circle and additional consonants to the larger circle when they are introduced in each lesson. See Figure 7.

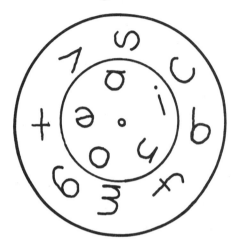

Figure 7

Another method that encourages smooth blending is to put the consonants on the smaller circle and the vowels on the larger circle. See Figure 8.

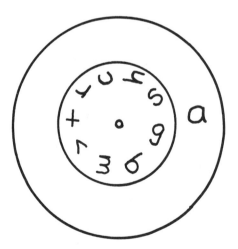

Figure 8

LESSON 12   *f*

is the cross kitten sound. It is continuous and to hear how it sounds, say the word *if* and *fish*. Its shape looks a bit like a "t" so you'll want to mention the curly top when you use the tactile letters.

1. "F" Words for Further Practice.
   A. Oral Practice
      fat, fall, fish, fun, father, fight, five
   B. On Board Practice
      fat, fast
2. Reading Activity for the "F" Sound—Newspaper Sounds.

   Give your child an old newspaper and a magic marker and have him circle all the "f"s he can find.

LESSON 13   *i*

is a vowel and can make several sounds, but the sound it makes most of the time is the i-i-i sound as in the words *it* and *in*. Its unique shape is the dot, and be sure to let your child trace the tactile letter with his finger.

1. "I" Words for Further Practice.
   A. Oral Practice
      Indian, igloo, is, it, if, in
   B. On Board Practice
      it, sit, hit, bit
      if
      him, big, fig
2. Reading Activity for the "I" Sound—Reading Wheels.

   Add the vowel "i" to the Reading Wheels you made in Lesson 11 by writing an "i" in the smaller circle. You can also add new consonants to the outer edge of the larger wheel.

LESSON 14   k

makes the same sound as "c." To hear this noncontinous sound say the words *kite* and *key*. Be sure to tell your child that "c" and "k" make the same sound and when they appear together we say "c" only once.

1. "K" Words for Further Practice.
   A. Oral Practice
      kit, kiss, king, kitten, kick
   B. On Board Practice
      kit, kiss, kick
      ask, tick
2. Reading Activity for the "K" Sound—Kite Making.

If the weather permits, make a simple kite out of construction paper and fly it outside with your child. If the weather is bad, draw a picture of a kitten and let your child color it.

LESSON 15   n

is a continuous sound and when you make "n" you can feel a slight vibration in your nose. Say the word *not*. Now say *run* and hold the n-n-n sound. Because of the similarity in shape, "n" is sometimes confused with "m." You can reduce some of that problem by mentioning that "n" has one hump. A word of caution here. When discussing each sound's unique shape never compare one shape to another and say something like, "The 'n' has one hump and the 'm' has two humps." Mentioning two similar letters at the same time doesn't clarify the confusion, it only adds to it. It's a bit like using oranges and apples to explain apricots, so stick with the characteristics unique to that letter.

1. "N" Words for Further Practice.
   A. Oral Practice
      nut, nose, night, net, not

B. On Board Practice
   nab, nag, nick
   in, tin, fin
   an, can, man, fan
2. Reading Activity for the "N" Sound—Treasure Hunt.

Write "n" on pieces of paper and hide them around the house. Encourage your child to find them and read the sound.

LESSON 16   *d*

is one of the first and most universal sounds babies make and apparently one clever dad cribbed this sound from mothers and thus "da da" came to mean father. "D" is not continuous and makes a single sound as in the words *had* and *dog*. Try to keep the sound as pure as possible and avoid adding vowel sounds when introducing it to your child.

1. "D" Words for Further Practice.
   A. Oral Practice
      dig, duck, daddy, dog, dress, dinner
   B. On Board Practice
      dig, dim
      ad, bad, sad, had, dad
2. Reading Activity for the "D" Sound—Finger Tracing.

Pour a thin layer of Cream of Wheat onto a cookie sheet. Show your child how to trace a "d" in the Cream of Wheat with his finger. Erase the "d" by gently shaking the cookie sheet.

LESSON 17   *l*

is a sound many children can hear but cannot say correctly. Young children often lack the motor control to get their tongues up behind the upper front teeth and many times the difficulty doesn't clear up until the second or third grade. So don't get upset if your child's l-l-l comes out more like a ya-ya-ya. To hear the "l" sound say the words *lip* and *fill* aloud. The sound of "l" is continuous and when blending "l" be sure to keep your tongue up behind your teeth before proceeding on to the next sound.

1. "L" Words for Further Practice.
   A. Oral Practice
      leg, love, lip, lap, lollipop, lake, lid, lad
   B. On Board Practice
      lag, lit, lad, lid
      lick, ill, fill, hill
2. Reading Activity for the "L" Sound—Lollipop.

   Give your child a lollipop to lick. Be sure to mention that lick and lollipop begin with the "l" sound.

LESSON 18   o

is a vowel and the sound it makes most of the time is o-o-o as in *ox* and *octopus*. When you introduce this sound to your child get a mirror and let him see how his mouth rounds when he says o-o-o.

1. "O" Words for Further Practice.
   A. Oral Practice
      ox, octopus, ostrich, opera
   B. On Board Practice
      rot, hot, dot, not, tot, got
      nod, rod, sod
      mom
2. Reading Activity for the "O" Sound—Reading Wheels.

   Add "o" to the Reading Wheels you made in Lesson 11 by writing an "o" in the smaller circle. You can also add new consonants to the outer edge of the larger wheel as they are introduced.

LESSON 19   p

is the puffing sound. To hear "p" say the words *hop* and *pig*. "P"
is sometimes confused with "d" or "b" so be sure to let your child
trace the "p" tactile letter card.

1. "P" Words for Further Practice.
   A. Oral Practice
      pop, pig, pot, pan, popcorn, pie
   B. On Board Practice
      pop, pot, pan, pig, pat, pin
2. Reading Activity for the "P" Sound—Popcorn.

   Let your child help you pop and eat some popcorn.

LESSON 20   e

is perhaps the hardest vowel to pronounce. To hear the "e"
sound, say the words *ever* and *Ed*.

1. "E" Words for Further Practice.
   A. Oral Practice
      Ed, ever, end, elk
      On Board Practice
      end, elk, ten, nest, help,
      get, let, pet, set, bet
2. Reading Activity for the "E" Sound—Reading Wheels.

   Add the vowel "e" to your Reading Wheel.

LESSON 21   x

sounds a bit like a drop of water on a hot stove, "ks." Actually "x"
is two sounds combined. To hear the "x" sound say the words
fox and *ax*.

1. "X" Words for Further Practice.
    A. Oral Practice
        ax, tax; ox, box, fox; six, fix
    B. On Board Practice
        ax, tax; fix, six; fox, box, ox
2. Reading Activity for the "X" Sound—Treasure Hunt.

Write the letter "x" on pieces of paper and hide them around the house. Encourage your child to find them and read the sounds.

LESSON 22   J

is a continuous sound and to hear it say the words *jump* and *jam*. Because of the dot, "j" is sometimes confused with "i."

1. "J" Words for Further Practice.
    A. Oral Practice
        jam, Jello, jeep, jump, jet, joke
    B. On Board Practice
        jet, jam, jip
2. Reading Activity for the "J" Sound—I'm Thinking of Something.

Tell your child that you're thinking of something that begins with the "j" sound. Give simple clues to describe the object such as "it shakes," "it melts in your mouth," "it is cold," etc. (Answer —Jello.)

LESSON 23   u

is a vowel and makes several different sounds, but the sound it makes most frequently is the u-u-u sound as in *up* and *umbrella*. Practice making the sound aloud and the "u" sound should sound a bit like the sound we make when we stammer—uh-uh-uh.

1. "U" Words for Further Practice.
    A. Oral Practice
        up, us, under, umbrella
    B. On Board Practice
        us, up, cup; duck, luck
        lump, bump, jump; fun, bun
        hut, cut; just
2. Reading Activity for the "U" Sound—Reading Wheels.

    Add the vowel "u" to your Reading Wheels.

LESSON 24   w

is the sound of the wind, w-w-w. It is continuous and to hear it
say the words *will* and *with*.

1. "W" Words for Further Practice.
    A. Oral Practice
        wet, wig, win, wish, window, work
    B. On Board Practice
        wet, wig, win, went
2. Reading Activity for the "W" Sound—Newspaper Sounds.
    Give your child an old newspaper and a magic marker and
have him circle all the "w"s he can find.

LESSON 25   y

is a part-time consonant and part-time vowel and the sound it
makes depends upon its relationship to other letters in the word.
In this book "y" is introduced first as a consonant, as in *yellow*
and *yes*, and later as a vowel as in sticky and funny.

1. "Y" Words for Further Practice.
    A. Oral Practice
        yes, yo-yo, yellow, yuck, yell

B. On Board Practice
    yes, yuck, yell
2. Reading Activity for the "Y" Sound—Letter Necklace.

Write "y" on a small piece of cardboard and string it on a piece of yarn or shoelace. Let your child wear the letter necklace and ask him a few times throughout the day what sound the letter makes.

LESSON 26   z

is the buzzing of the bee sound. It is continuous and to hear the z-z-z sound say the words *zip* and *zebra* aloud.

1. "Z" Words for Further Practice.
    A. Oral Practice
        zebra, zip, zipper, zero, zoo, zap
    B. On Board Practice
        zip, zap
2. Reading Activity for the "Z" Sound—Finger Tracing.

Pour a thin layer of Cream of Wheat onto a cookie sheet. Show your child how to trace the letter "z" in the Cream of Wheat with his finger. Erase the "z" by gently shaking the cookie sheet.

LESSON 27   qu

is a two-letter sound. (These will be discussed in more detail in Chapter Six.) To hear the "qu" sound say the words *queen* and *quit*. Try not to say "qua" and keep the sound as pure as possible.

1. "Qu" Words for Further Practice.
    A. Oral Practice
        quit, queen, quilt, quack, quiet

B. On Board Practice
quit, quilt, quack

2. Reading Activity for the "Qu" Sound—I'm Thinking of Something.

Tell your child that you are thinking of something that begins with the "qu" sound. Give simple clues to describe the object such as "she wears a crown," "she lives in England," etc. (Answer—queen.)

LESSON 28   *Teach the Sounds of the Uppercase Letters*

Your child will probably need more practice identifying letters in uppercase type (A,B,C, etc.). Here are a few exercises to include in your reading program to help him learn the sounds of the letters in uppercase type:

1. Make a set of uppercase tactile letter cards for A,B,C,D,E,F, G,H,I,J,K,L,M,N,O,P,Qu,R,S,T,U,V,W,X,Y,Z. Play matching games and pair these cards with the set of lowercase tactile letter cards you made in Chapter Two.
2. Use flash cards, alphabet posters, wall charts or any learning material where the uppercase and lowercase letters appear together and go over the sounds of the letters with your child.
3. Make alphabet puzzles and help your child match the uppercase and lowercase letters. See Figure 9.

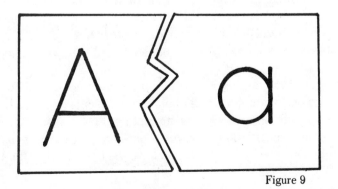

Figure 9

LESSON 29   Teach Names: Daisy & Macadoo

Even though sight words won't be formally taught until Lesson 36 it's a good idea to teach your child to identify the names of the comic strip characters Daisy and Macadoo because their names will appear in many of the following comic strips. Simply write their names on a blank sheet of paper, point to each word, and tell your child, "These words say, 'Daisy, Macadoo.'" Do this a few times throughout the day until your child can identify their names on his own.

Setbacks

Despite our best efforts we all have those dismal days when we run hot, and the child runs cold, and all the talk about the r-r-r sound and the m-m-m sound holds for our prodigy all the thrill and excitement of the hiccups. On those off-days when your child has memory lapses, he daydreams, or when he scratches or yawns incessantly, remember:

DON'T TEACH ANYTHING NEW, JUST REVIEW!!!

Heaven knows it's going to be hard enough plowing through the sounds he knew yesterday (or thought he knew yesterday), much less tackling new sounds today.

If you can get through a quick review fairly painlessly, then either dismiss class and hope for a better tomorrow or opt for a change in routine.

A change in routine can be anything from holding class in a different room to reading a silly story, to a letter treasure hunt, to making pretzel letters from frozen bread dough, to blowing bubbles, to whatever your imagination and inclination conjures up.

One fun way to break with routine and perk up your child's tired blood without boiling yours is to exchange roles and let the child be the teacher. Playing student not only gets you off your feet, but because no one approximates your teaching behavior closer than your own child, you have the unique opportunity to observe a facsimile of your own behavior—the good, the bad, and the ugly. And once you really act out the role of student and exchange chairs, chalk, lessons, and responsibility with your child, you can learn a lot about how you teach and possibly think of ways to improve on your teaching skills.

While you play "student" and your child plays "teacher" ask yourself a few questions:

1. Are his instructions clear and precise? If not, he may not understand the material himself.

2. Is his teaching style cheerful and enthusiastic, or dry and humorless? Guess whom he learned that from.

3. Make a mistake on purpose. Does he scowl and scold and give you the third degree or are corrections handled quickly and without anxiety?

4. Give the correct answer. Does he hug, kiss, or praise or are correct answers taken for granted?

Children enjoy playing teacher and rarely pass up the chance to "be teacher" because it affords them that rare opportunity to be in control and to tell their parents what to do without fear of repercussions. For you, playing student is a rare opportunity to examine the relationship between you and your child, and when you're hoping for a lifetime of peaceful coexistence, that's certain to be food for thought.

SUMMARY OF ASSIGNMENTS FOR CHAPTER FOUR

1. Play a rhyme game with your child for a week.

2. Practice the listening games Slow Poke and Word Division a few minutes each day for the next week.

3. Play Follow-the-Arrow with your child each day for the next week.

4. Complete Lessons 1 through 29 with your child and teach him how to read.

Comic Strips for Lesson 4

LESSON 1 *m*

m–m–m

m–m–m

Panel 1. Daisy and Macadoo are cooking. Look at how neat and clean the kitchen is.

Panel 2. Daisy lets Macadoo taste some batter from a spoon. It tastes good and they both say, "*M-m-m.*"

Panel 3. Daisy and Macadoo are happy about the delicious cupcakes they baked. They say, "*M-m-m.*" But look at the kitchen—it's a mess!

LESSON 2   *t*

t–t–t

t–t–t

t–t–t

Panel 1. It's late at night and Daisy and Macadoo are in bed.
They are trying to go to sleep, but the clock is
ticking too loudly. It goes, "*T-t-t.*"

Panel 2. It's gotten even later and they still
can't get any sleep. The clock goes, "*T-t-t.*"

Panel 3. Then Daisy gets an idea. She throws
her pillow over the clock.

Panel 4. Now the clock is ticking softly, and
now Daisy and Macadoo can sleep. "*T-t-t.*"

LESSON 3   *s*

S–S–S

S–S–S

S–S–S

Panel 1. Daisy and Macadoo are pretending
to be snakes. They say, "S-*s-s.*"

Panel 2. Daisy and Macadoo stop playing because
they hear something else saying, "S-*s-s.*"

Panel 3. Why it's a silly snake who's pretending to
be a person—*s-s-s.*

LESSON 4 *b*

b–b–b   b–b–b

Panel 1. Macadoo is flying over the ocean and he spots something that looks like a worm. It goes, "*B-b-b.*"

Panel 2. Macadoo wants to eat the worm for lunch and he pulls hard. But the worm won't budge. It just goes, "*B-b-b.*"

Panel 3. Daisy appears and is she mad. The "worm" Macadoo wants to eat is her snorkel!

Panel 4. Daisy gives it to Macadoo all right—and she wraps the snorkel around his beak. Poor Macadoo!

r–r–r   r–r–r

Panel 1. Macadoo is not being very nice. He's chasing after a little kitten and roaring, "*R-r-r.*"

Panel 2. The kitten runs to his father—a huge lion. The father lion is mad and he roars, "*R-r-r.*"

Panel 3. Now it's Macadoo who's running scared.

m–m–m

C–C   C–C

Panel 1. A cat puts a fish in his mouth.

Panel 2. Out comes a clean bone. The cat says, *"M-m-m."*

Panel 3. Daisy and Macadoo want to eat fish the same way the cat does but . . .

Panel 4. The fish gets caught in their throats and out it comes with a *"C-c-c-c."*

LESSON 7   *g*

Panel 1. A frog catches a fly.

Panel 2. He swallows it with a "*G.*"

Panel 3. Lots of flies fly by and the frog tries to eat them all.
He goes, "*G-g-g.*"

Panel 4. The frog ate all the flies, but his tongue got tied in knots.
He feels a little sick and says, "*G.*"

LESSON 8 *h*

h-h-h-h

Panel 1. Daisy and Macadoo are having a picnic. Everything is nice and pleasant until . . .

Panel 2. Some silly bugs come jogging by saying, "*h-h-h-h.*"

Panel 3. They stop eating and ask, "What was that!" Tell me what sound were those bugs making?

a

a-a-a

a

a

Panel 1. Daisy is teaching Macadoo the "*a*" sound.

Panel 2. Macadoo wants to learn how to read, and he writes, "*a-a-a*" on everything he sees . . .

Panel 3. He even writes "*a*" on some of his friends . . .

Panel 4. Including Daisy! "A."

LESSON 10 v

V–V–V   V–V–V

V–V–V

Panel 1. Daisy and Macadoo watch a big jet that says, "V-*v-v*."

Panel 2. Macadoo tells Daisy that he can do that too, and he flies up in the sky and says, "V-*v-v*."

Panel 3. A real jet comes and Macadoo tries to get out of its way—"V-*v-v*."

Panel 4. Macadoo barely escapes, but he lands safely in a tree.

fat ham

fat rat

bam

m–m–m fat ham

Panel 1. Daisy is slicing a *fat ham*.

Panel 2. A *fat rat* appears and wants some ham.

Panel 3. Daisy hits the fat rat. *Bam!*

Panel 4. Now Daisy eats the ham. She says, "*M-m-m fat ham.*"

hit it

hit it hit it

bam

bit it

Panel 1. Daisy is playing golf. Macadoo tells her, *"Hit it."*

Panel 2. Daisy is getting nervous. Macadoo shouts louder, *"Hit it, hit it!"*

Panel 3. Daisy hits the golf ball with a *bam.*

Panel 4. Macadoo and the golf ball land on the green. Daisy hit the ball, and Macadoo *bit it.*

kick it

big kicks

kiss him

big kiss

Panel 1. Macadoo is mad and he wants to *kick it*.

Panel 2. Macadoo is still angry and he gives everybody some *big kicks*.

Panel 3. A rabbit comes along to *kiss him*.

Panel 4. The *big kiss* made Macadoo stop feeling mad.

in

in

in

fat fit

Panel 1. Daisy throws a toy *in* a pool.

Panel 2. She throws more toys *in*.

Panel 3. Daisy jumps *in*.

Panel 4. The pool is too full. It is a *fat fit*.

dig

dig

can

m-m-m   ick

Panel 1. Daisy watches Macadoo *dig*.

Panel 2. Macadoo continues to *dig*.

Panel 3. Macadoo finds a *can*. It is a *can* of worms.

Panel 4. Macadoo says, "*M-m-m*." Daisy says, "*Ick*."

m-m-m

lick

licks

big lick

Panel 1. Macadoo is licking an ice cream cone. He says, "*M-m-m.*"

Panel 2. Daisy asks for a *lick.*

Panel 3. Daisy *licks* the ice cream right off the cone.

Panel 4. It was a *big lick.*

hot

hot

not hot

Panel 1. Daisy is at the beach.

Panel 2. The sun is *hot*.

Panel 3. Daisy gets too *hot*.

Panel 4. Macadoo cools her off with some water.
Now Daisy is *not hot*.

p

pop

pop pop pop

m-m-m it pops

Panel 1. Macadoo hears something go, *"P."*

Panel 2. The *"pop"* comes from an ant hill.

Panel 3. The ant hill goes, *"Pop, pop, pop."*

Panel 4. Macadoo takes a peek. He says, *"M-m-m it pops."*

nest

big nest   help

Panel 1. Macadoo wants to . . .

Panel 2. Build a *nest*

Panel 3. He builds a *big nest*.

Panel 4. The next is too big. Macadoo gets stuck and he screams, "*Help!*"

fix it

ax

mad

bam fix him

Panel 1. Daisy takes her car to the service station and asks the attendent to, "*Fix it.*"

Panel 2. The attendent uses an *ax* to fix the car.

Panel 3. Daisy returns and she is *mad*. The man did not fix her car.

Panel 4. *Bam!* Daisy decides to *fix him!*

v-v-v   jet

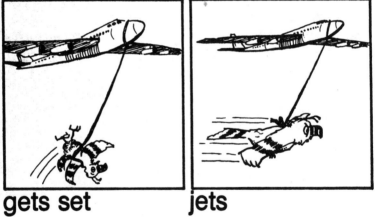

gets set   jets

Panel 1. Macadoo watches a jet approach. "V-v-v."

Panel 2. Macadoo wants to catch the *jet*.

Panel 3. He *gets set*.

Panel 4. Now there are two *jets*.

up

up

big jump

big bump

Panel 1. Some little animals jump *up*.

Panel 2. Daisy jumps *up*.

Panel 3. She takes a *big jump*.

Panel 4. She comes down with a *big bump*.

wig

wet wig

wets wig

wet wig

Panel 1. Macadoo combs Daisy's *wig*.

Panel 2. Daisy asks Macadoo to *wet wig*.

Panel 3. Macadoo *wets wig*.

Panel 4. It is too wet. It is a *wet wig*.

yuck

yuck yuck

yes

yuck

Panel 1. Daisy works as a waitress in a restaurant. She brings the goat a roast chicken. The goat says, "*Yuck.*"

Panel 2. Daisy brings a pizza and Macadoo brings him a hamburger. But the goat says, "*Yuck, yuck!*"

Panel 3. Daisy brings the goat a menu so he can order something else. The goat says, "*Yes.*"

Panel 4. The goat eats the menu. Daisy says, "*Yuck!*"

zip it

zip

zips

zap

Panel 1. Daisy asks Macadoo to, "*Zip it.*"

Panel 2. Macadoo tries to *zip* the dress but it's not easy.

Panel 3. Macadoo *zips* the dress.

Panel 4. But look at Daisy. She's been zapped. *Zap!*

quick

duck

quack quack

Panel 1. Macadoo flies down *quick*.

Panel 2. He finds a *duck*. He pulls the string . . .

Panel 3. The duck goes, "*Quack, quack*." He likes the duck.

Panel 4. On no! The duck is a toy.

FIVE
Joy of Reading

You're at the halfway mark in this program and if your child is deciphering simple words, recognizing letter sounds, or simply more enthusiastic about learning, you deserve a round of applause. But while you're taking credit for those remarkable changes in your child, stop and consider any concurrent changes taking place in you.

A Japanese philospher said, "To teach is to learn," and teaching a child to read is that and more. It is a chance to grow and share, to touch and laugh, to amaze and be amazed, and to transcend the daily tedium of dirty dishes, yellow wax build-up and ring-around-the-collar commercials. As one mother concluded, "It is a chance to assist in a miracle."

But alas, teaching a child to read, like most real life miracles, seldom follows the smoothly ticking precision of a Cecil B. De Mille production, and in your role as miracle worker you've probably encountered any number of questions or problems that have made you hesitant or unsure and kept you from reaching your full potential as a teacher. Not always knowing the answer is as natural in the teaching process as in the learning process, and this chapter discusses many of the problems common to parents who teach, and perhaps answers some of the problems you have encountered.

THE TRUTH ABOUT TEACHING YOUNG CHILDREN

Teaching young children to read is a delightful experience that typically requires little more than enthusiasm and a fundamental approach to learning as a game. The trick to teaching young children successfully is not so much in correcting deep-seated problems as in preventing them from developing, and here are some warning signals to look out for:

1. *Short attention spans*

Although you'll have extraordinary days when enthusiasm and interest are high and when your sessions can run up to an hour, generally young children cannot sit still and pay attention for longer than fifteen or twenty minutes. And when your child starts fidgeting or looks plain bored, that's your cue to end the lesson.

Dr. Dorothy Strickland, professor of education at Columbia University, says, "Asking young children to sit for long periods of time devoted to rote, abstract learning is asking for trouble . . . it is wiser to adapt the method to the child rather than attempt to do it the other way."[1]

One way to adapt this teaching program to the child with a short attention span is to divide the lessons into smaller segments than I have done already. Instead of holding one daily fifteen- or twenty-minute session, why not hold two daily eight-minute sessions or one daily ten-minute session?

Of course I should mention that there is a lower limit that operates here and if you should decide to teach only five minutes per day, it is questionable how much real learning can take place. Furthermore, you haven't really solved the basic problem of how to help your child develop a longer attention span, and that's something to consider if your child is about to start school, because kindergarteners are usually required to sit still for longer

1. Strickland, D. "Take Part in a Miracle—Help Your Child Learn to Read," *Early Years Magazine*, 1980, *11*, p. 5.

than ten minutes. Increasing a child's attention span is a gradual but not too difficult process, and here are a few tips.

- Read stories aloud to your child.
- Attend plays, concerts, and puppet shows together.
- Play some of the attention-span-building games in Chapter Three such as: Lids and Bottles, Painless Puzzles, and Lotta-Lotto.
- Encourage your child to listen to children's records (these are available at public libraries).

2. *Forgetting a sound*

Forgetting a sound or confusing one sound with another is a common mistake among young children, and most parents find it somewhat bewildering that the same child who can recite television jingles verbatim can't tell the difference between "d" and "b." When your child gets stuck on a sound or can't seem to master a lesson as quickly or as competently as he had previous ones, don't attempt to hammer or drill the information into his head until he finally "gets it." Instead, move more slowly and painstakingly through the lesson, review the key elements of the lesson, and then move on to a new sound. Some sounds *are* harder to remember than others and you can still get good teaching results if you include brief review activities for the "troublesome sound" in your regular teaching schedule. Here are some ways to deal with forgetting and errors.

- After you've gone through the lesson once, break it down into one- to three-minute segments and teach them as mini-lessons throughout the week(s).
- Refer to the reading activities in Chapter Four, Lessons 1 through 29, and look for reading games that can serve as review exercises for the "troublesome sound."
- Draw your child's attention to words on cereal boxes, traffic signs, menus, billboards, and store signs which contain the letter your child is having difficulty learning.

- Be patient and persistent, and if you don't let a backlog of troublesome sounds build up, your child will eventually learn the sound.

THE TRUTH ABOUT TEACHING TWO OR MORE CHILDREN

For parents with children around the same age and for anyone responsible for educating two or more children, teaching everybody at the same time is often the only practical method for teaching every child who wants to read how to read.

The Good News: Learning together as a group can foster team spirit and camaraderie and result in a richer and fuller reading experience for each child.

The Bad News: Young children have a natural affinity for solo performances, and getting them to work together with a combined sense of purpose and direction can try the diplomatic talents of even a Kissinger.

Assuming you'd prefer your teaching session be a joy and not a wrestling match, here are a few suggestions.

1. *Limit the group size*

Continual and immediate feedback is essential for good reading instruction and in order to keep your finger on every pulse, you'll need to limit the size of your class. If you've had no prior teaching experience I suggest you start off with no more than three students at one time. If you've taught groups of students before, I suggest teaching no more than six children at once.

2. *Good organization counts: Structure lessons*

When you teach one-on-one the advantage is yours and quite often the sheer momentum of a teacher's enthusiasm can compensate for any shortcomings. But teaching more than one child requires more structure and better organization, because if you don't know what to do and where you're going, you can bet your gang will come up with a few novel ideas of its own. To keep your sense of direction (and your sanity) I suggest you 1) write out your lesson plans at least one week in advance and keep them together in a bound notebook, 2) make all learning games in advance and store them in a permanent storage area, and 3) use graphs, charts, or written notes to keep track of each student's individual progress. Be sure to include information on the lessons covered, the sounds mastered, and the sounds left to teach.

3. Individualize

Teaching the group as a whole while meeting the needs of each student is the challenge for every good teacher. One way to accomplish both is to allot time for individual instruction as well as for group instruction within your regular teaching schedule. For instance, group instruction can last ten minutes or fifteen minutes and be a time to introduce new lessons and review old lessons. Individual instruction time can be in five-minute periods, disseminated throughout the day, to help each student with oral reading, troublesome sounds, or whatever.

4. Control behavior

Getting students to pay attention and respond on cue can be done by using the behavior modification techniques outlined in Chapter Two. Review that chapter for insight into how to correct discipline problems.

THE TRUTH ABOUT TEACHING OLDER CHILDREN

Unlike the young child who starts these lessons with an unprejudiced mind and a naïve acceptance of reading as a game, the older child already in school has seen and experienced enough failure to know better; and even the pep of a Dallas Cowgirl isn't enough to "turn on" a child who has "tuned out," because his problems tend to be psychological as well as academic. But obstacles can be overcome. Remember, Albert Einstein didn't talk until he was three. Even Bruce Jenner flunked second grade. And every day children labelled dyslexic, retarded, or just plain hopeless win the battle against illiteracy and learn to read. Here are some of the problems associated with teaching older children, and ways to help:

1. *Easily discouraged*

Quite often children who have experienced repeated failure won't even attempt to try again. It's simply too painful. As his teacher, it's your job to penetrate this barrier and convince your child that he can learn. One way of doing this is to start your lessons by teaching him easy material that he already knows. For example, if your child already knows some consonant sounds, teach the ones he knows, first. If he can recognize names of family members, friends, pets, etc., teach those as sight words before trying other words. In your attempt to build success into your teaching program, don't be afraid to be unorthodox and break the rules, including the ones provided here, because any success your child enjoys now can develop into a habit for success in reading later.

2. *Guessing at words*

Even children who learned to read the phonics way can't resist the occasional temptation to guess a word rather than to sound it out, but for older children having trouble learning to read, the temptation to guess is more like a compulsion. To keep your reading session from becoming a game of chance with every word up for grabs, remember one rule: Don't Allow Guessing!

Make your child use his decoding skills to unlock the pronunciation of each word. Ask him to give you the sound of each letter in the word. If he gives you all the sounds in the word (or all the sounds with your assistance) and still doesn't recognize the word, then you should tell him what the word is.

3. *Use humor*

Humor is the perfect antidote for alleviating the anxiety and frustration older children feel when they try to learn and can't. When your child starts to struggle through a particularly difficult lesson or sentence, instead of encouraging him on, stop occasionally and take a moment to talk humorously about your own foibles and goofs in life. Perhaps you can mention the time the car ran out of gas on the expressway, or the time you misread a cake recipe and substituted salt for sugar, or the time you flunked your driver's license exam and had to bum a ride home. The topic of your particular blunder doesn't matter as much as the timeless and comforting message it conveys: that fear, failure, and "blowing it" are a part of the human experience we all share.

A PARENT'S BILL OF WRONGS

Somebody once said, "Power tends to corrupt and absolute power corrupts absolutely." While you may not totally agree with this observation, it is hard to dispute the basic premise that power can be dangerous. Now that you've placed yourself in the powerful and precarious role of both parent and teacher, here are a few imaginary tongue-in-cheek consequences to consider the next time your Napoleon Bonaparte streak starts showing:

1. *Obscenity*

Children who are forced to recite alphabets for visiting relatives, read labels for grocery store clerks, or participate in similar acts of exhibitionism are granted one telephone call to their attorneys.

2. *Child Abuse*

Parents who make insulting remarks such as, "You knew

that yesterday, why don't you know it now?" are to be dismissed from class and required to sing from memory all four stanzas of the national anthem.

3. *Telephone Calls*

Telephone conversations are illegal during teaching periods. Parties to the crime shall be placed on a nine-and-a-half-month hold and learn what it is to wait.

4. *Foul Play*

Parents who withhold answers, rush through lessons, pass over praises, and otherwise engage in foul play shall be relieved of their teaching duties and re-assigned as television game show hosts or coaches for the NFL.

5. *A Declaration*

Students who are obstructed from progress, deprived of love, and generally fatigued and overtaxed are hereby authorized to declare war and their independence.

SIX

Teaching Multiple Letter Combinations

Now that you've whetted your child's appetite for reading and have taught the basic twenty-six sounds of the alphabet, it's time to go a step further and teach multiple letter combinations —the sounds various letters make in combination with each other. To do that, let's first discuss some of the terminology reading teachers and linguists use to describe multiple letter combinations. (I hope this vegetable soup lingo doesn't make your eyes blur, but I believe that thinking through these terms will help you understand and teach multiple letter combinations effectively.)

Digraphs. Digraphs are two consecutive letters that jointly make a single speech sound. Digraphs are read as a unit and the individual letters cannot be separated and read phonetically. Common digraphs include the consonant digraphs sh, th, wh, ch (as in shoe, thread, wheel, church) and the vowel digraphs ow, oo, ee, au (as in blow, soon, flee, naughty).

Diphthongs. Diphthongs are two consecutive letters making a single sound by sliding the sound of the first letter into the sound of the second letter. Common diphthongs include oy, ue, ou (as in boy, blue, out).

R-controlled Letters. When the letter "r" follows a, e, i, o, and u, the regular sound of the vowel is changed and instead of making a separate vowel sound, the vowel makes a single sound in conjunction with the "r." Examples of r-controlled letter combinations are ar, or, er, ur, and ir (art, for, herd, turn, stir).

Phonograms. Phonograms are a cluster of consecutive letters that begin with a vowel. Phonograms are often referred to as word families and some common phonograms are ight, ang, ink, and ing.

Word Endings. Word endings are attached to the end of a word and are commonly referred to as suffixes. Some of these terms are interchangeable: for instance, "ing" is a phonogram and a word ending.

Learning to read multiple letter combinations is more difficult than learning to read single letters because the child has to recognize two (and sometimes three) letters as a single sound unit. Consequently, you'll need to introduce multiple letter combinations at a slower rate than the single letters and you can probably expect your child to master only one or two multiple letter combinations per week.

To help you accomplish a feat which can make even trained teachers' heads spin, I have summarized the basic six-step reading format you used in Chapter Four and have included a step-by-step format for teaching multiple letter combinations.

THE BASICS

The teaching format for multiple letter combinations is essentially the same six-step procedure you used in Chapter Four to teach single letter sounds. Here is an outline of the six-step reading format, along with comments about the difference between teaching single letter combinations and multiple letter combinations.

Six-Step Reading Format	Basic Changes for Teaching Multiple Letter Combinations
STEP 1. Assemble your teaching materials.	You'll need both white and colored chalk.
STEP 2. Review old sounds.	No change.
STEP 3. Use the chalkboard and tactile letter cards to introduce the new sound.	Make a set of lower-case tactile letter cards for each MLC.
STEP 4. Practice words that contain the new sound: orally, on the chalkboard, and with Language Center pictures.	Color-code the MLC words that you write on the chalkboard.
STEP 5. Read the comic strip to your child.	No change.
STEP 6. Play reading games.	No change.

THE PROCEDURE

To get a more specific idea of how to teach multiple letter combinations I have detailed a suggested procedure. Keep in mind that the format presented here, like your basic recipe, is only a guideline. You have to supply the necessary ingredients of warmth, humor, affection, and discretion to get the texture and flavor you like.

Lesson—Teaching "Th"

STEP 1   Gather your materials: the chalkboard, chalk (both white and colored), tactile letter cards, Language

Center pictures, comic strips, and materials for the reading activity.

STEP 2 Review old sounds.

STEP 3a Write "th" on the chalkboard. Use lower-case letters. Point to the letters and say, "These letters say 'th.' What sound do these letters make?"
Child answers, "Th."
I like to begin any discussion on multiple letter combinations by first explaining why these letters have changed their sounds. I tell my children that we're going to learn about some letters that are friends; and when these friends come together they forget the sound they normally make and instead, make a new sound together. And my children, with their gift for fantasy and fabrication, find this irrational explanation quite plausible. You can, of course, feel free to invent any fairy tale your children will swallow.

STEP 3b Hold up the "th" sandpaper letter card. Say, "These letters say 'th.' What sound do these letters make?"
Child answers, "Th."
Encourage the child to examine the sandpaper letter with his finger.

STEP 4a Oral Practice. Select about three to five words from the "Oral Practice Word List" in Lesson 30 of this chapter. Ask your child to listen for the "th" sound in each word and to repeat each word after you.

STEP 4b Locate pictures in the Language Center which begin with the "th" sound and share these pictures with your child. You could introduce the pictures by saying something like, "Let's talk about some things that begin with 'th.'"

STEP 4c   On Board Practice. With a few variations, these steps are the same blending steps you learned in Chapter Four, Lesson 11. See Figure 10a,b,c,d,e.

1. Draw a large horizontal arrow on the chalkboard.

Figure 10a

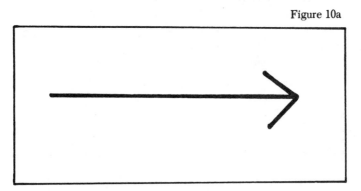

2. Use colored chalk to write "th" on top of the arrow. This color coding technique helps a child discriminate between the multiple letter combination and the other letters in a word. It's a good idea to color code each new word you introduce. As your child becomes more familiar reading multiple letter combinations within a word you can eliminate the color code technique.

3. Point to the "th" and ask your child what sound the letters make. (Child says "th.")

Figure 10b

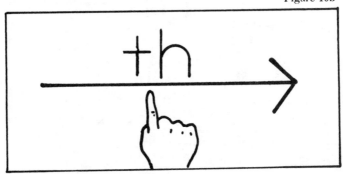

4. Use white chalk to write "at" next to "th" and make the word "that."

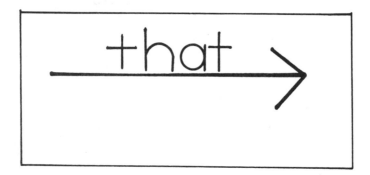

Figure 10c

5. Ask your child to say each sound you touch and to listen for the word the sounds make.

6. Point to "th." (Child says "th.") Be sure to place your finger between the letters and not to point to any particular letter.

Figure 10d

7. Slide finger over to "a" and then to "t." (Child says "a-a-t.")

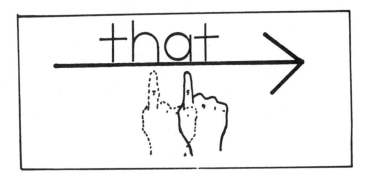

Figure 10e

8. Go back and underscore the letters with your finger as you slowly say, "thaat."

9. Ask your child what the word is. If he says "that," hug, kiss, and act very pleased. If he doesn't say "that" then give him the answer and say "that."

10. Practice blending the word "that" a few more times. Encourage your child to read "that" by himself.

11. Refer to the "On Board Practice Word List" in Lesson 30. Select a few more words and help your child read them.

STEP 5   Read the "Th" comic strip to your child.

STEP 6   Reading Activity. Refer to the Reading Activity section of Lesson 30 for a game to play with your child.

Now that you've gotten some ideas how to teach multiple letter combinations, it's time to talk about a few assignments.

Assignments #1, 2, and 3

Your first assignment for this chapter is to read Lessons 30 through 55 and practice making each sound.

Assignment #2 is to make a set of tactile letter cards for each multiple letter combination. Make the letters either all felt or all sandpaper. Here is the list of MLC's you'll need tactile letter cards for:

th, ee, ing, sh, wh, oo, ar, ch, or, ay, igh, ow, al, er, ou, ur, ol, aw, ir, kn, oy, wr, oi, ew, y

Assignment #3 is, of course, to start teaching!

THE MULTIPLE LETTER COMBINATION LESSONS

LESSON 30　　*th*

is a consonant digraph that represents two distinct sounds: 1) "th" a voiced sound as in *mother, the, bathe*; and 2) "th" a voiceless sound as in *tooth, thumb, cloth*.[1] Lip and tongue placement for making both sounds are identical—the tongue goes between the teeth. A common mispronunciation is to place the tongue over the bottom lip and make the "f" sound.

Because the voiced "th" is used in many common words (that, them, with) and because children whose native tongue is English usually have little trouble learning when to apply the correct "th" sound to a word, you'll teach the voiced "th" sound in this lesson. Once your child becomes familiar reading words containing the voiced "th" sound, you can teach the voiceless "th" sound in words such as *thin, path, bath,* etc.

---

1. To feel the difference between voiced "th" and voiceless "th," touch your throat and say bathe (voiced) and tooth (voiceless).

1. "TH" Words for Further Practice.
   A. Oral Practice
      that, the, they, this, mother, brother, breathe
   B. On Board Practice
      this, them, that, then
2. Reading Activity for the "TH" Sound—Spin-A-Word.

   Fasten a cardboard arrow to the center of a cardboard circle. Use a paper fastener or screw and nut. Write "th" on the point of the arrow and write "is," "em," "at," "en" around the outer edges of the cardboard circle. See Figure 11. Show your child how to turn the "spinner" to make words.

Figure 11

LESSON 31   ee

is a vowel digraph and to hear the "ee" sound say the words *seed* and *tree*. The double "e" makes the same sound as long "e."

1. "EE" Words for Further Practice.
   A. Oral Practice
      eek; keep, jeep, sleep
      green, wheel; see, bee, three, coffee

B. On Board Practice
   eek, jeep, keep, peep, sleep; seen, green
   weed, seed, need
   see, bee, tree, three
2. Reading Activity for the "EE" Sound—Plastic Tab Scramble.

Collect plastic tab fasteners from bread and produce bags. With a laundry marker, write "ee" on one tab. Write consonant letters on the remaining tabs (b,c,d,f,g,h,j,k,l,m,n,p,qu,r,s,t,v,w, x,y,z). Help your child combine the plastic tabs to make different words. Refer to the on board practice word list for examples. See Figure 12.

Note: The comic strip for this lesson contains words in which the final "s" sounds like "z." If this confuses your child, explain that sometimes "s" sounds like "z" at the end of a word.

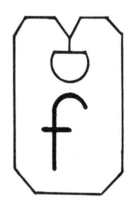

Figure 12

LESSON 32   ing

is a phonogram and a word ending. In the words *sing, wing, thing,* etc., the "ing" is used as a phonogram. In the words *jumping, going,* and *sewing,* the "ing" is used as a word ending. Some areas of the United States don't stress the "ing" ending. When a double consonant precedes the "ing," only one double consonant is read.

1. "ING" Words for Further Practice.
   A. Oral Practice
      going, cutting, kissing, jumping, bringing
      sing, wing, king, thing, bring
   B. On Board Practice
      sing, ring, king, wing, thing
      helping, jumping, kissing, digging, filling
2. Reading Activity for the "ING" Sound—Mountain Climber.

Draw a stepped mountain slope on the chalkboard or on a large sheet of paper. Write word beginnings such as "r," "w," "k," "th," "br," on each step. Cut out an "ing" mountain climber from a separate sheet of paper. Move the mountain climber from step to step and have the child try to read each word the mountain climber comes to. See Figure 13.

Figure 13

LESSON 33   *sh*

is a consonant digraph and is often referred to as the keep quiet sound or the hush sound. To hear the "sh" sound say the words *fish* and *shop*.

1. "SH" Words for Further Practice.
   A. Oral Practice
      shop, shoe, shot, sheet, shut, shell, ship
      push, fish, dish, wish, crash, trash
   B. On Board Practice
      shop, shut, ship, shell, shack
      fish, dish, wish; rush, brush; cash, flash, trash
2. Reading Activity for the "SH" Sound—Little Bo-peep.

Draw and cut out several pictures of sheep. Put the sheep under various objects around the house that begin with "sh" such as sheet, shoes, shutters, shovel, shells, and toy ships. Tell your child that Little Bo-peep has lost her sheep and can't tell where to find them. Ask your child to help Little Bo-peep find her sheep and to look for sheep under objects around the house that begin with the "sh" sound.

LESSON 34   wh

is the sound of the big wind and the "wh" sound is really "wh" pronounced backwards, "hw." To hear the "wh" sound say the words *whip* and *which*. A common mispronunciation is to confuse "wh" with the "w" sound. To see how much more air blows out when you say "wh" than when you say "w," hold up your hand to your lips and say both sounds. In some regions of the U.S., "wh" and "w" are pronounced as the same sound, so use the "wh" pronunciation that suits your locality.

1. "WH" Words for Further Practice.
   A. Oral Practice
      whip, whale, wheel, white, where, when
      wheat, whistle
   B. On Board Practice
      whip, when
2. Reading Activity for the "WH" Sound—Shoe Box Match.

Glue several small pictures that begin with "wh" onto a cardboard rectangle or shoe box lid. Now glue several pictures that do not contain "wh" onto the same cardboard rectangle. Give your child several cardboard circles with "wh" printed on them and have him match the "wh" circle to the "wh" picture. Examples of a few words where pictures might be easily found include: whip, whale, whistle, wheat, and wheel.

LESSON 35   oo

is a vowel digraph and one of the more difficult letter combinations to teach because the letters "oo" make two distinct sounds: "oo" as in *boot* and in the hooting of an owl, and "oo" as in *good*. Of the two sounds, the "oo" as in *boot* is the primary sound and it is used in about 59 percent of the most common words containing the "oo" letter combination.

Unfortunately, even though "oo" as in *boot* is the dominant sound throughout our language, "oo" as in *good* is frequently found in children's beginning readers. Remember "Look Jane look." And even the vocabulary-controlled Dr. Seuss beginner book *The Foot Book* uses the minor sound of "oo" throughout the text. However, in these lessons you'll be teaching the primary sound of "oo" (as in *boot*) and here are a few suggestions for getting around the confusion of who is "oo":

- Teach the "oo" sound as in *boot* and teach the words *took, look, foot,* and *cook* as sight words. (Sight words are covered in the next lesson.)
- First, teach the "oo" sound as in *boot* and teach the minor sound of "oo" as in *good* after you complete the last lesson in this chapter.
- Whatever you do, don't teach both "oo" sounds at the same time, because with all the different "o" letter combinations your child can get confused.

1. "OO" Words for Further Practice.
   A. Oral Practice
      boot, food, moon, pool, tooth, too, room
   B. On Board Practice
      boot, cool, pool, fool, tool
      room; moon, soon, spoon
      too, shampoo, igloo
2. Reading Activity for the "OO" Sound—Go Fish.

   Make a "fishing pole" by tying a magnet onto a small stick with a piece of string. Make a set of "oo" word cards by writing the words "boot," "too," "spoon," "room," etc., on separate cardboard squares. Fasten paper clips onto the word cards and place in a pail or box. Give your child the fishing pole and let him "go fishing" for "oo" words in the pail. Allow him to keep each word he can read. See Figure 14.

Figure 14

LESSON 36   *Sight Words*

Sight words are irregular words which follow no phonetic pattern or no easily decodable phonetic pattern. Sight words are different from the other words your child has learned because they need to be automatically recognized "on sight" and without phonetic analysis. Most children's books use a standard sight word vocabulary, and here is a list of words commonly found in early readers that don't sound out or follow phonic rules your child has learned.

come	put	want	for	we
of	here	where	I	a
there	were	your	good	some
to	you	look	said	they
work	saw	he	away	little
the	was	go	and	on

Your child's further reading progress is contingent upon his mastering many of the words on this list. While there are no hard and fast rules for effectively teaching sight words, here are a few good approaches:

1. As with multiple letter combinations, sight words take longer to learn than single letter sounds. There are more letters and fewer clues to how the word sounds. To show your child that a basic decoding technique can be applied in varying degrees to all words,[2] demonstrate on the chalkboard which parts of the irregular words do and do not sound out.
   a. One way to do this is to write the word on the chalkboard and color code the irregular parts.
   b. Another way is to write the irregular word on the board and put happy faces near the regular letters and sad faces near the irregular letter(s).

2. The word OF is the exception—it doesn't sound out.

2. Because memory and repetition are keys in reading sight words, many teachers and parents use learning games to make the drilling less tedious and more palatable. Among the games parents choose are:

   a. Flash Cards. Write words one inch high or larger on index cards or cardboard rectangles. Allow one word per card. Hold up the card, read the word, and ask the child to repeat the word.

   Variation 1. Using the same words, make another set of flash cards. Hold up your flash card and ask the child to find the flash card in his stack that matches yours.

   Variation 2. Mix up the flash cards. Have the child find and read the matching pairs.

   Variation 3. Jump the Hurdle. Lay a path of sight word cards on the floor. Have your child jump from one card (hurdle) to the next as he reads each word correctly.

   b. Sentence Grab Bag. Include the sight words in simple sentences written on strips of paper. Allow one sentence per strip. Fold the strips and put in a paper bag. Shake the bag and have the child pull out a strip and read the sentence. Some examples of simple sentences are, "He ran fast," "A cat can jump," and "This pig is fat."

   Variation. Take Directions. Use the sight words in simple sentences that give directions. Some examples are, "Put the hat in a bag," "Sit on the rug," and "Stand next to me."

   c. Word Search. Have your child locate and circle any sight words appearing in newspapers, magazines, bulletins, and various other printed literature.

   d. Informal Learning Activities. Encourage your child to find sight words on road signs, posters, logos, traffic signs, menus, etc.

Assignment #4. Teaching Sight Words

Make sight word activities part of your regular reading program. Introduce about two or three sight words per week and use any or all of the aforementioned approaches to teach them. (You can also include names of family members, pets, colors, numbers, street names, etc.)

LESSON 37   *ar*

is an r-controlled letter combination. To hear the "ar" sound say the words *farm, arm,* and *card, hard.*

1. "AR" Words for Further Practice.
   A. Oral Practice
      arm, art, armor
      farm, alarm, harm
      hard, card; park, bark, shark
      car, star, far, jar
   B. On Board Practice
      arm, art; hard, card; shark, dark, park
      jar, car, far, star
2. Reading Activity for the "AR" Sound—Picture Pieces.

   Locate a picture of an object whose name contains "ar," such as *arm, shark, car, star.* Glue the picture onto a sheet of paper. Print the name of the object at the bottom of the sheet. Divide paper into separate strips by cutting between the sounds in the word printed at the bottom. (See Figure 15, and be sure not to divide "ar.") Mix up the pieces and ask your child to arrange the strips into a complete picture and to try and read the word at the bottom.

Figure 15a

Figure 15b

LESSON 38   *ch*

is a consonant digraph and two distinct sounds are generally associated with the "ch": 1) the primary sound of "ch" as in *chop* and as in a train starting off (choo-choo), and 2) the minor "ch" sound as in *chord* ("ch" makes a "k" sound). The primary sound occurs in about 63 percent of all "ch" letter combinations, and you'll teach the "ch" sound as in *chop* in this lesson.

The "sh" and "ch" sounds are often confused.

1. "CH" Words for Further Practice.
   A. Oral Practice
      chop, chair, chain, chest, chimp
      match, pitch, march, ranch, teach
   B. On Board Practice
      chop, chip, cheek, chug, chest
      rich, much, match, crunch, catch
2. Reading activity for the "CH" Sound—Reading Wheels.

Join two cardboard circles, one larger than the other, with a screw and nut or paper fastener. Write "ch" on the outer edge of the smaller circle and write "ip," "op," "est," "eek," on the outer edge of the larger wheel. See Figure 16. Show your child how to turn the wheels to make words.

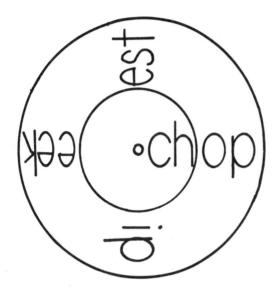

Figure 16

LESSON 39   *or*

is an r-controlled letter combination. To hear the "or" sound, say the words *organ* and *corn*.

1. "OR" Words for Further Practice.
    A. Oral Practice
        or, for, door, corn, born, short
        fork, stork, storm, porch
    B. On Board Practice
        or, organ
        for, fork, pork; corn, born, torn
2. Reading Activity for the "OR" Sound—Talking Bird.

Draw a picture of a parrot on the chalkboard and draw a large cartoon bubble above the parrot's head. Write "or" inside the bubble and draw one blank along each side of "or." See Figure 17. Make the parrot "talk" and say words by filling in the blanks with different letters. Refer to the "On Board Practice List" above.

Figure 17

LESSON 40   *ay*

is a vowel digraph and it makes the long sound of the vowel "a" as in the words *day* and *say*.

1. "AY" Words for Further Practice.
   A. Oral Practice
      day, say, gay, clay, play, ray, gray, Sunday
   B. On Board Practice
      day, say, ray, gay, may, ray, lay
      play, clay, gray .
      Sunday, payment
2. Reading Activity for the "AY" Sound—Plastic Tab Scramble.

   Collect plastic tab fasteners from bread and produce bags. With a laundry marker, write "ay" on one tab. Write consonant letters on the remaining tabs. Help your child combine sounds to make different words.

LESSON 41   *Igh*

is a vowel digraph and this letter combination makes the sound of the long "i" as in the words *right* and *high*.

1. "IGH" Words for Further Practice.
   A. Oral Practice
      high, sigh
      right, fight, might, tight, light
   B. On Board Practice
      high, sigh
      right, fight, might, tight, light
      slight, bright
2. Reading Activity for the "IGH" Sound—Flip-A-Word.

   Make a word-flip chart for the "igh" sound from a three-ring notebook binder. Write beginning consonant sounds (br, f, h, m, n, r, s, sl, t) on small cardboard rectangles and attach them to the first ring in the binder. Write "igh" on a small rectangle cardboard and attach it to the second ring. Write ending consonant sounds (t, ts) on small cardboard rectangles and attach them to the third ring. See Figure 18. Also include a blank rectangle on the third ring. Have the child flip through the various letters to see if he can make a word.

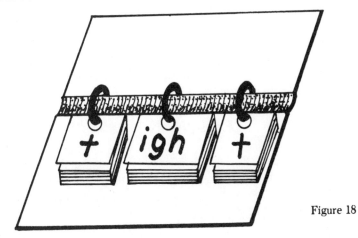

Figure 18

LESSON 42   ow

can be either a diphthong or a vowel diagraph. In the words *owl*, *now*, *cow*, *brown*, etc., "ow" is a dipthong that is read by sliding the "o" sound into the "w" sound. In the words *own*, *grow*, *low*, etc., "ow" is a vowel digraph that is read as the long "o" sound. Since both sounds are commonly used, it's a good idea to familiarize your child with both "ow" sounds. You can do this by explaining to him that "ow" makes two sounds and when he comes to a word containing "ow," first to say each sound separately. If saying each sound separately fails to unlock the pronunciation of the word, then try reading "ow" as in a long "o."

Although this lesson concentrates on the "ow" sound as in *grow*, you'll probably need to give your child some practice reading words with "ow" as in *cow*. (Now, flower, brown, etc.)

1. "OW" Words for Further Practice.
   A. Oral Practice
      own, low, row, blow, flow, grow, throw
   B. On Board Practice
      own; grown, shown
      low, row, blow, crow, slow, throw
2. Reading Activity for the "OW" Sound—Concentration.

Paste pictures of objects whose names contain "ow" on index cards. (Elbow, pillow, yellow, shadow, window, crow.) Paste pictures of objects whose names do not contain the "ow" sound on another set of index cards. Lay both sets of cards picture side up and have your child try to match one "ow" card with another "ow" card.

LESSON 43   al

is a letter combination in which the "l" can change the sound of "a." To hear the "al" sound that is taught in this lesson say the words *salt*, *always*, *tall*. (Words which are common exceptions include *alley*, *Al*, *alligator*.)

1. "AL" Words for Further Practice.
    A. Oral Practice
        all, always, also, salt, fall, ball, walrus
    B. On Board Practice
        all, tall, fall, ball, call, hall, wall
        salt, bald
2. Reading Activity for the "AL" Sound—Color-the-Letter.

Draw a dotted outline of "al" on an 8 in. by 10 in. sheet of paper. Have your child "color" the "al" sound by gluing dry beans, macaroni, cotton, yarn, etc., to the dotted outline. See Figure 19.

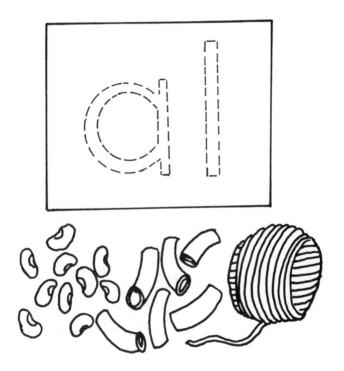

Figure 19

LESSON 44 *er*

is an r-controlled letter combination and part of the "bossy r" trio in which the letter "r" controls the sound of the vowels "i," "e," and "u"; so instead of making a separate vowel sound, the vowels all make the same "er" sound in conjunction with the "r." To hear the "er" sound say the words *faster* and *her*. Some areas of the United States don't stress the "er" sound at the ends of a word, so adapt the "er" sound at the end of words to fit your locality.

1. "ER" Words for Further Practice.
   A. Oral Practice
      bumper, fixer, her, herd, faster, under, mother
   B. On Board Practice
      er, her, per, fern, herd
      helper, bumper, fixer, jumper
      after, ever, under
2. Reading Activity for the "ER" Sound—Plastic Tab Scramble.

   Collect plastic tab fasteners from bread and produce bags. With a laundry marker, write "er" on one tab. Write consonant letters on the remaining tabs (b, c, d, f, g, h, j, k, l, m, n, p, qu, r, s, t, v, w, x, y, z). Help your child combine the plastic tabs to make "er" words. Refer to the "On Board Practice" word list for examples. See Figure 20.

Figure 20

LESSON 45   *ou*

is a diphthong and to hear the "ou" sound, say the words *out* and *cloud*. (Another letter combination makes the same sound, "ow" as in owl.) The "ou" sound is part of a larger group of letter combinations beginning with "o"—"oo," "ow," "oa"; and because these letters all look and sound somewhat alike, your child may get a bit confused.

1. "OU" Words for Further Practice.
   A. Oral Practice
      out, shout, found, sound, loud, cloud, about
      mouse, house
   B. On Board Practice
      out, loud, cloud, shout, count
      found, sound, round, hound
      house, mouse, blouse (These last three have a silent "e"; use your own discretion on whether or not to teach.)
2. Reading Activity for the "OU" Sound—Coat Hanger Mobile.

Write "ou" words on index cards and suspend from a coat hanger. Hang the coat hanger mobile from the ceiling in your child's room and help your child read the words.

LESSON 46   *ur*

is an r-controlled letter combination in which the "r" controls the sound of the vowel. To hear the "ur" sound, say the words *urn* and *hurt*.

1. "UR" Words for Further Practice.
   A. Oral Practice
      urn, turn, burn; curb, hurt, curl
   B. On Board Practice
      urn, burn, turn; hurt, curb, curl
      church, burst, Thursday

2. Reading Activities for the "UR" Sound—Go Fish.

Make a "fishing pole" by tying a magnet onto a small stick with a piece of string. Make a set of "ur" word cards by writing the words *burn, curl, turn,* etc., on small, separate cardboard squares. Fasten paper clips onto the word cards and place in a pail or box. Give your child the fishing pole and let him "go fishing" for "ur" words in the pail. Allow him to keep each word (fish) he reads.

LESSON 47   ol

is a letter combination in which the "l" controls the sound of the "o." To hear the "ol" sound say the words *hold* and *roll.* Notice that the "o" is long.

1. "OL" Words for Further Practice.
    A. Oral Practice
        old, cold, fold, sold, told, gold
        pole, hole, mole, stole
        roll, toll, loll
        colt, holster
    B. On Board Practice
        old, cold, sold, told, fold
        colt, bolt, roll, toll, poll
        pole, hole, mole, stole (Even though the silent "e" rule won't be formally discussed until Chapter Seven, your child will probably be able to sound out these words if you tell him the "e" is silent.)
2. Reading Activity for the "OL" Sound—Flip-A-Word.

Make a word-flip chart for the "ol" sound from a three-ring notebook binder. Write beginning consonant sounds on small cardboard rectangles and attach them to the first ring in the binder. Write "ol" on a small rectangle of cardboard and attach to the second ring. Write ending consonant sounds (d, t, l) on small rectangles and attach them to the third ring. Have the child flip through various letters to see if he can make a word.

LESSON 48   *aw*

is a vowel digraph. To hear the "aw" sound say the words *awful* and *saw*. Another letter combination making the "aw" sound is "au" (auto, autumn, sauce).

1. "AW" Words for Further Practice.
   A. Oral Practice
      awful, saw, jaw, raw, draw
      hawk, straw, shawl, claw, outlaw
   B. On Board Practice
      law, jaw, raw, paw, saw, thaw
      hawk, straw, crawl, shawl, claw
      outlaw
2. Reading Activity for the "AW" Sound—Puzzle Pieces.

Write words containing "aw" on separate index cards. Cut each card into two- or three-piece puzzles. Be sure not to divide "aw." See Figure 21. Ask your child to fit the puzzle pieces together and to read the word.

Figure 21

LESSON 49   Ir

is an r-controlled letter combination in which the "r" controls the vowel sound. To hear "ir," say *sir* and *birth*.

1. "IR" Words for Further Practice.
   A. Oral Practice
      sir, stir
      dirt, shirt, flirt
      girl, bird, birth, first, third, skirt, thirst
   B. On Board Practice
      sir, dirt, girl, bird
      shirt, birth, flirt, stir, thirst
2. Reading Activity for the "IR" Sound—Flip-A-Word.

Make a word-flip chart for the "ir" sound from a three-ring notebook binder. Write consonant sounds on small cardboard rectangles and attach them to the first ring in the binder. Write "ir" on a small cardboard rectangle and attach to the second ring. Write consonant sounds on cardboard rectangles and attach to the third ring. Have your child flip through the various letters to see if he can make a word.

LESSON 50   kn

is a consonant digraph and makes the same sound as the letter "n." Listen for the "kn" sound in these words: *knee, knock, knit.*

1. "KN" Words for Further Practice.
   A. Oral Practice
      knee, knit, knock, knob, knife
   B. On Board Practice
      knit, knob, knee, knock
2. Reading Activity for the "KN" Sound—Shoe Box Match.

Glue several small pictures that begin with "kn" onto a cardboard rectangle or shoe box lid. Now glue several pictures that do not begin with "kn" onto the same cardboard rectangle. Give your child several cardboard circles with "kn" printed on them and have him match the "kn" circle to the "kn" picture.

LESSON 51   oy

is a diphthong and the "oy" letter combination makes the same sound as the "oi" letter combination. To hear the "oy" sound, say the words *joy* and *oyster*.

1. "OY" Words for Further Practice.
   A. Oral Practice
      boy, joy, Roy, toy, cowboy
   B. On Board Practice
      joy, toy, boy, Roy, oyster
2. Reading Activity for the "OY" Sound—Bean Bag Toss.

Write several "oy" words on separate index cards. Lay the word cards on the floor. Ask your child to toss a bean bag at the word cards and to identify the word it lands on.

LESSON 52   wr

is a consonant digraph and the "wr" sound makes the same sound as the letter "r." To hear the "wr" sound, say the words *wrap* and *write*.

1. "WR" Words for Further Practice.
   A. Oral Practice
      wrist, wreck, wrong, wrap, wrinkle, wrestle, wrench

B. On Board Practice
   wrist, wrap, wreck, wrench
2. Reading Activity for the "WR" Sound—Reading Circles.

Join two cardboard circles, one larger than the other, with a screw and nut or paper fastener. Write "wr" on the outer edge of the smaller circle and write "ap," "eck," "ench," "ist," on the outer edge of the larger wheel. Show your child how to turn the wheels to make words.

LESSON 53   *oi*

is a vowel digraph and to hear the "oi" sound, say the words *oil* and *poison*. The "oi" sound makes the same sound as "oy" and they are frequently taught as twin sounds. Margaret McEathron, in her book *Your Child Can Learn to Read*, says that "oy" is usually at the end of a word, and "oi" is usually in the middle of a word because in our language we don't like to end a word with an "i," so instead we write "oy."

1. "OI" Words for Further Practice.
   A. Oral Practice
      oil, boil, soil; join, coin
      noise, point, moist, voice, poison
   B. On Board Practice
      oil, soil, boil; join, coin
      point, moist, spoil
2. Reading Activity for the "OI" Sound—Bean Bag Toss.

Write several "oi" words on separate index cards. Lay the word cards on the floor. Ask your child to toss the bean bag at the word cards and to identify the word it lands on.

LESSON 54   ew

is a vowel digraph and to hear the "ew" sound, say the words *new* and *shrewd*. Other multiple letter combinations making this sound are "oo" (chew/choo) and "ue" (blue, Sue).

1. "EW" Words for Further Practice.
   A. Oral Practice
      new, few, dew, threw, stew
      shrewd, grew, flew, chew
   B. On Board Practice
      new, few, chew, drew, flew, threw
2. Reading Activity for the "EW" Sound—Talking Bird.

   Draw a picture of a parrot on the chalkboard and draw a large cartoon bubble above the parrot's head. Write "ew" in the bubble and draw a blank line along each side of "ew." Make the parrot "talk" and say words by filling in the blanks with different letters.

LESSON 55   y

is both a vowel and a consonant. I call it "changeable y" because it makes so many sounds, either alone or in combination with another letter. With young children you may want just to introduce the long "e" sound of "y" as in *funny*, and merely mention that the other sounds for "y" will be covered later. With older children you may want to go over some of the various sounds "y" makes:

a. Long "e" sound. When "y" is at the end of a two or three syllable word it usually makes the long "e" sound. Some examples are *funny, baby, candy, pretty, hurry*. ("Ey" can also make the long "e" sound—*key, turkey*.)

b. Long "i" sound. When "y" is at the end of a one syllable word it usually makes the long "i" sound. Examples include *cry, fly, my, why, sly, try*.

c. Short "i" sound. The "y" can also make the sound of "i" as in *gym, myth*.

1. "Y" Words for Further Practice (long "e" sound).
    A. Oral Practice
        baby, candy, pretty, hurry, bunny, funny
    B. On Board Practice
        pretty, hurry, candy, funny, bunny
2. Reading Activity for the "Y" Sound—Coat Hanger Mobile.

Write words ending in the long "e" sound of "y" on index cards. Suspend the cards from a coat hanger mobile and hang the mobile from the ceiling in your child's room.

SUMMARY OF ASSIGNMENTS FOR CHAPTER SIX

1. Read Lessons 30 through 55 and practice making each sound.

2. Make a set of tactile letter cards for each multiple letter combination.

3. Teach Lessons 30 through 55 to your child.

4. Make sight words part of your regular reading program.

Comic Strips for Lesson 6

this can fit

with this

with that

it fits

Macadoo sees
this tree

Macadoo
peeks in

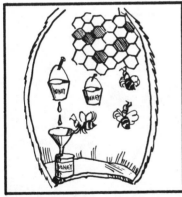

Macadoo sees
bees

now Macadoo
flees

bending

jumping

singing

cracking

Macadoo is
mad Daisy will
not help

now Macadoo
will not help

this ship will
crash

Lets rush past

Macadoo has
fun tricks

but when
Macadoo
cracks his whip

whack

Macadoo gets
this big kick

Macadoo
shoots pool

this dog shoots
too

Macadoo
shoots fast

Macadoo
shoots too fast

this darn car
will not start

Macadoo gets
some parts

this is a

smart start

New Sight Words:
a
some

LESSON 38   *ch*

m-m-m lunch

chop chop and

crunch crunch

Daisy had too
much lunch

New Sight Words:
and

it is a storm
Daisy and
Macadoo can
not sleep

they grab the
sheet and

rip

New Sight Words:
they
the

the sheet is
torn it is a
short sheet

lets play with clay

Macadoo gets a tray of clay

and sprays

wow

New Sight Words:
of

Macadoo sees
a fight

it is not right to
fight

Macadoo stops
the fight

whack

New Sight Words:
to

Daisy plays
with snow

Macadoo
throws snow

Daisy is mad

Daisy blows
the snow

No New Sight Words

this fish needs
salt

Daisy adds
some salt

this fish is still
not all right

this walrus is
all wet

No New Sight Words

Macadoo sees
a jumper and
a helper

and a sleeper

Macadoo
wants to kiss
her but beep

this sleeper is
a beeper

New Sight Words:
wants

out

get out of
this can

come out
now

ouch

New Sight Words:
out

surfs up
get out

Macadoo turns

and curls

and hurts

No New Sight Words

hold this ball   roll it

the ball bumps   and left big
and rolls   holes

No New Sight Words

Macadoo can draw

Daisy has a big yawn

Daisy is mad at what she saw

the drawing is a big jaw

New Sight Words:
what
she

lets start girls   this is first

this is second
and third and

crash
that stuff
is for the birds

New Sight Words
do

Daisy knits   Macadoo knits

lots of knots

Macadoo has
fun knocking
the ball

No New Sight Words

thats a good
boy

now boy

get this toy

oh boy that is
not a toy

New Sight Words:
oh
good

wrap this gift
sir

h–m–m this
seems right

he wraps fast
and

wraps her wrist

New Sight Words:
he

Macadoo adds
oil to the mix

it boils

he wants
Daisy to
join in

yuck

No New Sight Words

Macadoo
and Daisy
chew gum

Daisy blew
and blew until

her bubble
pops

Macadoo said I
knew it

New Sight Words:
I
said

m–m–m
Macadoo licks
candy

Daisy asks for
a lick

her lick is
tricky but

this candy is
sticky

No New Sight Words

SEVEN

Moving Into Books

Learning to read is like learning ballet, piano, or tennis in that proficiency is acquired through a series of initially slow, awkward, and sometimes painful steps. To help your child progress from clumsy deciphering into the smooth assimilation we call reading, you'll need to transform your at-home reading program from one that emphasizes sounds, blending, and word patterns into one that concentrates more on comprehension, accuracy, and vocabulary.

How exactly are you going to do this?

Quite simply, you can help your child grow as a reader by getting him started reading books. Books to laugh about, think on, cry over, and fall asleep with. After all, isn't that why you started teaching these lessons in the first place?

Books have characteristics that make them different and perhaps more difficult than the reading your child has done. Below is a list of some of the peculiarities found in books that tend to create problems for a beginning reader.

Variations in print type style. The letters a, g, and a few others are printed and written differently. If your child has been reading billboards, menus, newspaper headlines, etc., he has probably somewhat reconciled the variations in print type style; however, if your child hasn't done much reading outside the Daisy and Macadoo comic strip, you probably need to teach him the different print types, particularly for the letters "a" and "g." You can demonstrate different print types for the same letter by using flash card drills, on board examples, matching games, or wall charts.

Variations in print type size. The print in books, even in many easy-to-read books, is small, and requires the reader to have highly developed visual discrimination skills. Therefore, when you select books for your child to read, select easy-to-read books with large print so that he can see what he's reading.

Punctuation. There is a whole host of punctuation marks that your child will eventually have to make peace with, but the ones that appear with stubborn regularity even in easy-to-read books are periods, commas, question marks, exclamation points, and apostrophes. Fortunately, many children, particularly those who have been read to a great deal, already have a built-in sensitivity to pauses, stops, and expressed emotion within a sentence, and for most children a simple explanation on how each punctuation mark works will suffice.

Capitals. Capital letters start sentences and proper names, and if your child appears to have trouble reading words containing capital letters you might want to review the lowercase and uppercase matching exercises in Chapter Four, Lesson 28.

Other special features of books. Now that your child is ready to read books, it's a good time to acquaint him with or re-acquaint him with the location of the title, the title page, page number, and author's name. Most children enjoy being able to read a book's title or author's name even when that's the only part of the book they can read with confidence.

READING FOR MEANING—
DEVELOPING COMPREHENSION

Poor comprehension is common among beginning readers and, to a degree, the problem is aggravated by the beginning reading instruction itself.

What happens is that the typical sound-oriented beginning reading program requires a child to concentrate a great deal of his mental energy on sounding out or decoding words. Some children become so absorbed in and attentive to the mechanical process of giving the precise pronunciation and sound that they don't listen to the word or think about its meaning in relationship to the other words on the page. Consequently, it's not unusual for some children to read a passage with great artistry and draw a blank when someone asks them a question about what was read.

But there is no need for this to happen to your child. With a few simple techniques and some information on reading comprehension, you ought to be able to prevent comprehension problems from cropping up now.

How to Develop Reading Comprehension

Reading comprehension—the ability to understand what is read—is usually explained by dividing the subject into two areas: literal comprehension and non-literal comprehension. Literal comprehension is information that is explicitly stated in the story. It's the who, what, when, and where facts stated in the story and read directly off the page.[1] Here is a passage along with some typical literal comprehension questions that require the reader to supply the who, what, where, and when.

A mother cat and her five kittens went to the park one sunny afternoon. They walked up a high hill and slid down the other side of the hill. Then they went home.

1. The how and the why can also be considered literal information if those facts are stated directly in the story and require no interpretation on part of the reader.

1. Who is this story about? (a mother cat and her five kittens)

2. What did they do? (they walked up a hill and slid down the other side)

3. Where did this happen? (at the park)

4. When did they go to the park? (one afternoon)

But the retrieval of information is not the only reason we read. Quite often reading means not only finding the facts but intrepreting the facts, and this synthesizing of information is a higher level of reading comprehension called non-literal comprehension. Here is a passage, along with some questions that require the reader to make inferences, predict outcomes, and come up with conclusions that are not available directly through the story:

A little rabbit sat alongside a riverbank. The rabbit said, "It is getting dark. I want to get to the other side of this river." But the rabbit could not swim, so he sat and sat. A big turtle was going to the other side of the river. The turtle told the rabbit, "Come with me." The turtle took the rabbit to the other side of the river and the rabbit did not get wet.

These are some non-literal interpretive questions that might be asked about the story.

1. Why do you think the rabbit wanted to get to the other side of the river? (he wanted to get home before dark; he wanted to visit a friend before it got too late)

2. How did the rabbit feel when he could not get to the other side of the river? (sad; unhappy)

3. Was the turtle good or bad? Why do you think so? (he was good because he helped the rabbit)

4. How did the turtle take the rabbit to the other side of the river? (he carried the rabbit on his back; he used a boat)

5. If the turtle hadn't come along, how could the rabbit have gotten to the other side of the river? (he could have built a boat; hopped on a log and paddled; asked someone for help)

Although question-asking is the most common way to develop and test for comprehension, asking a beginning reader still struggling with smooth blending and sight-word identification a lot of questions about what he has read may not always be desirable or practical. Therefore here are some other techniques that develop comprehension for you to consider:

1. Re-tell the story. You can get a general feel for just how well your child comprehends what he reads by asking him to tell you about the story he has read. As your child re-tells the story, listen for what he remembers, understands, and considers to be the key elements of the story. If his re-telling indicates he understands very little of what was read, you can help by

- selecting easier reading material for him;
- showing him how to develop a story as a sequence of chronological events. For instance, as he re-tells the story, ask him what happened first, what happened second, what happened next, and so on.

2. Draw a picture. Even the child who can't clearly express himself in words can often respond with some imagination and creativity if asked to draw a picture about the story. And although the scratches and scribbles of a preschooler may seem rather primitive to you, the draw-a-picture technique teaches a child to narrow down the particulars of a story and actually introduces him to a higher level of reading comprehension—summarizing the main idea.

3. Puppetry. The use of puppetry to tell the story is essentially a creative variation of the re-tell the story technique. For ideas on how to conduct simple and quick puppet shows refer to Game 28 (Finger Puppets), Game 29 (Popsicle Stick Puppets), and Game 30 (Fist Puppets) in Chapter Three.

Assignment #1. Vocabulary Development

Research has shown a relationship between word knowledge and reading and thinking ability, and consequently, children with extensive vocabularies are not only the best readers, but they tend to be the best thinkers. What happens is that their efforts to define the world with clearer and more precise language enable them to perceive the world with sharper, active, and more insightful minds.

To help your child understand the words he'll encounter in his reading, as well as communicate his thoughts intelligently, it's wise to make vocabulary development part of your at-home reading program.

Other than talking to your child, perhaps the easiest and most obvious way to build your child's vocabulary is to continue to read to him. Books that make good reading for his age group include fairy tales, fables, humor books, animal stories, picture dictionaries, and information books on science, the fine arts, nature, and hobbies.

Two good reference books on selecting books for children are Nancy Larrick's classic *A Parent's Guide to Children's Reading* and a newer book, *Choosing Books for Children: A Commonsense Guide* by Betsy Hearne.

Another way to improve your child's vocabulary is through word games. Several vocabulary-building games are mentioned in Chapter Three. They include Ann's Antonym Match, Lotta-Lotto, Stacia's Synonym Match, and Word Painting.

Your first assignment for this chapter is to make vocabulary building part of your at-home reading program. Use any or all of the aforementioned methods, and if you lack time to teach vocabulary development, encourage other members of your family to share the responsibility or consider hiring a local schoolgirl to come in and help.

BOOKS YOUR CHILD CAN READ NOW

While there is a wealth of good books available for children who can already read well, there are still too few good books for children at the just-beginning-to-read or primer stage.[2] However, there are many books your child can read now and here are some good, reasonably priced, easy-to-read books currently on the market:

1. *Just-Beginning-to-Read Books* by Margaret Hillert. Published by Modern Curriculum. This series includes fifty-six storybooks, with some readers containing easy-to-read versions of children's classics such as *Little Red Riding Hood* and *The Three Bears*. Other notable features of the books in this series include: vocabulary lists, a controlled vocabulary that becomes increasingly more difficult, a parent's guide, and the availability of inexpensive paperback editions. These books are available through bookstores or public libraries.

2. *The Ladybird Books*. Published by Ltd. Loughborough. This series includes thirty-six easy-to-read storybooks, with many containing reading and writing activities. Other notable features of this series include large print type, full-color illustrations, workbooks, picture dictionaries, controlled vocabulary, vocabulary lists, and a parent's guide. *Ladybird Books* are available through bookstores and public libraries.

---

2. This situation is changing, so stay in touch with your bookstore and local librarian for the latest books.

3. A *First-Start Easy Reader* by Troll Associates. This series of easy readers is appropriate for beginning or remedial readers. Each edition depicts delightful characters in comical situations which young children may find appealing. The large type, controlled vocabulary, and simple sentences help young readers master each edition with relative ease. A word-for-word cassette tape of each book is also available. *First-Start Easy Readers* can be purchased through libraries and schools.

4. More Difficult Books. As your child becomes more proficient as a reader you'll probably want to introduce him to some of the more advanced easy-to-read books. Two popular series include Troll's *I Can Read* series and Random House's *Beginner Books*. Both series are available in libraries, bookstores, or through children's books clubs at discounted rates.

5. Make a Book. Homemade books offer a unique, personalized touch to your child's reading experience as well as show him the reciprocal relationship between reading and writing. Homemade books can be made by binding or stapling some sheets of construction paper together along an edge, and the stories can be about the child, a family member, a pet, an imaginary character, or any of your child's special interests. Illustrations could be photographs, pictures cut from magazines, or even the child's own artwork. If you should decide to make a book, encourage your child to "play author" and let him write or dictate (to you) his own stories.

Assignment #2. Reading Sessions

Your second assignment for this chapter is to select one or two easy-to-read children's books (preferably consecutive books from the same reading series) and to conduct daily oral reading sessions with your child. In the beginning, limit the actual time your child is reading to only a few minutes and gradually increase the length of each session until he can read an entire book in one sitting.

Here are some teaching pointers you may find useful:

Before the session:

- Select easy-to-read books with large print type.
- Check the book's vocabulary. If 25 percent or more of the words are not either phonetically decodable or sight words your child has already learned, then the book is too difficult for your child, and you should select another one.
- Read the book to your child the day before he does so that he already knows how the entire story connects and flows.
- Introduce sight words or unfamiliar words on the board before the reading session begins.

During the session:

- Use a pencil to point to each sound the child reads aloud. As the child becomes a more accomplished reader you can eliminate this sound-by-sound technique.
- Keep a notebook handy and when your child comes to a word he is unable to read, write that word out in large letters. Perhaps if he can see the word in the larger print, he will be able to read it more accurately. However, if your child has major difficulty with a particular sound or word, give it to him quickly so that his reading flow isn't disturbed too much.
- Practice team reading in which you and your child alternate reading lines or pages.

After the session:

- Use one of the comprehension techniques previously mentioned.
- Have patience, and faith in your child's ability to read.

Assignment #3. Teaching the Alphabet

Up to now we have concentrated on teaching the sounds, rather than the names of letters because beginning reading instruction is not necessarily dependent upon knowing the name of each individual letter. However, your child is nearing the point where knowing the names of the letters of the alphabet can enhance his reading ability as well as help him develop writing and spelling skills.

Learning the alphabet is essentially memory work and after your child has read several easy-to-read books, your next assignment for this chapter is to teach him the names of the letters in the alphabet. You can use repetitive learning activities involving flash cards, alphabet poster cards, wall charts, alphabet books, etc. Whichever method you choose, here are a few "Do's" and "Don'ts."

DO:
- Teach only one or two letters at a time.
- Teach the letters in isolation from additional words and pictures as much as possible.
- Refer to the letters as the *names* of the letters.
- Teach the uppercase and the lowercase letters together.
- Help your child memorize which letters are vowels.
- Use supplemental fun-learning activities such as singing "The Alphabet Song."
- Include simple writing activities such as *trace the dotted letter* for children who exhibit an interest in writing letters.

DON'T:

- Teach the names of the letters with the same material you used to teach the sounds of the letters.
- Use commercial or homemade materials with lots of distracting pictures or words.
- Overuse configuration clues such as "h" looks like a chair, "c" looks like a cookie, etc.
- Feel compelled to go in alphabetical order because many letters that appear in sequence either look alike or have similar names.
- Say "a is for apple," "b is for ball," etc.

Assignment #4. Special Sound Patterns

It probably seems as though I'll never stop bombarding you with different sounds and new assignments. Well, now you can relax (a bit) and rest on your laurels. The next lessons and assignments are optional—well, almost. Let me explain.

Up to now you have taught your child the most common sounds, and many of the remaining lessons introduce less common sounds and special spelling rules which may contradict those your child has already learned. Teaching these lessons now may not be either desirable, because they can confuse beginning readers, or even necessary because your children often pick up sound variations in the natural course of reading books. So, instead of feeling compelled to teach every single phonetic sound pattern mentioned here, you might want to wait until your child has had further reading experience, and teach words containing these special sound patterns as sight words, or you might want to thumb through the remaining lessons and teach only the ones which you feel are appropriate for your child now.

As your child becomes a more accomplished reader, and as these sounds appear more frequently throughout his reading, you can refer back to these lessons. You can teach them the same way you taught multiple letter combinations, with oral examples, on board examples, and the reading comic strip.

LESSON 56   The Magic e Rule

When "e" is the final vowel in a word, the preceding vowel is usually long (i.e., it says its name) and the final "e" is silent. (A common exception is *have*. Teach as sight word.)

Some teachers like to demonstrate the "magic" of the final e and give on board examples of words before and after magic "e." For example: hop + e = hope

mad + e = made

Words for Further Practice

kite	tube	dime	slide
note	cake	late	rope
Pete	eve		

LESSON 57   Adjacent Vowels

When two adjacent vowels appear in a word or syllable, the first vowel is usually long and the second vowel is usually silent. An example of this rule can be demonstrated with the word *heat*. HEAT = Heat = Hēt

Words for Practice

rain	pie	meat	read
boat	eat	soap	pail

LESSON 58   Soft c

When "c" is followed by "e," "i," or "y" (cent, city, cycle) the letter "c" makes the "s" sound.

Words for Practice

cent	fancy	face	cinch
city	race	ceiling	fence

LESSON 59   Soft g

When "g" is followed by "e," "i," or "y" (gentle, giant, gypsy) the letter "g" often makes the "j" sound. (Common exceptions are *get, girl give.* Teach as sight words.)

Words for Practice
gel   magic   germ   ginger

LESSON 60   Open Vowels

When a, e, i, o, or u, is the last and the only vowel in a word (or syllable) it is usually long. Examples include *go, me, baby.*

Words for Practice

no	he	tiny
so	be	baby
go	me	duty
	we	

LESSON 61   ph

is a consonant digraph and the "ph" letter combination makes the same sound as the letter "f." To hear the "ph" sound say the words *phone* and *graph.*

Words for Further Practice
orphan, photo, trophy, alphabet, phone, dolphin[3]

---

3. Use the "OL" sound that fits your locality.

LESSON 62   ANK

is a phonogram and to hear the "ank" sound, say the words *sank* and *bank*.

Words for Further Practice
rank   spank   blank
tank   lank
thank   prank

LESSON 63   Ink

is a phonogram and to hear the "ink" sound, say the words *sink* and *pink*.

Words for Further Practice
wink   mink   shrink
link   rink
think   blink

LESSON 64   ed

is a word ending that shows something has already happened (past tense). The three sounds of "ed" are:

1. "t" as in *stopped*

2. "d" as in *wished*

3. and "ed," a separate syllable after words ending in "t" or "d," e.g., *wanted, tooted.*

Since many children can say the correct "ed" sound orally better than they can read it, Douglas Carnine, in his book *Direct*

Instruction Reading, suggests first letting the child practice "ed" orally before you teach him how to read it on paper. Here is a variation of a teaching method Mr. Carnine suggests:

Mother: "I'm going to make some words into 'ed' words and show that something has happened. When I finish I'll give you some words to make into 'ed' words so you can show that something has happened. Here goes: cook . . . cooked, play . . . played, fish . . . fished. Now you make this word into an 'ed' word . . . hop . . ."

Child: "Hopped."

Mother: "Fix."

Child: "Fixed."

Words for Further Practice
help   jump   stop   wish   want   wink   toot   slice

LESSON 65   *le*

When "le" is at the end of a word the "e" is silent and the "l" makes its most common sound—l-l-l.

Words for Further Practice
bubble	candle	rattle
little	uncle	twinkle
apple	bottle	puddle

LESSON 66   *es*

is a word ending and when you teach the "es" suffix you'll probably want to teach the word before "es" and after "es." For instance: tax + es = taxes

Words for Further Practice

tax	fix
kiss	buzz
mix	fox
wish	glass

ASSIGNMENTS FOR CHAPTER SEVEN

1. Make vocabulary-building part of your at-home reading program.

2. Conduct daily oral reading sessions with your child.

3. Teach your child the names of the letters in the alphabet.

4. Begin teaching special sound patterns. (Optional)

Comic Strips for Lesson 7

Daisy plays with a kite.

Macadoo takes the kite.

Daisy chases after them.

Macadoo is safe.

Macadoo looks out the window and sees rain.

He gets a bar of soap.

He goes out in the rain.

Macadoo waits to take a bath.

Daisy has cider for sale.

Henry wants to buy cider for three cents.

Daisy changes the price.

Now cider costs ten cents.

Macadoo has
magic tricks.

Out comes a
rabbit.

Out comes
another rabbit.

Out comes a
giraffe!

Daisy says her yo-yo can go fast.

Macadoo says his yo-yo can go faster.

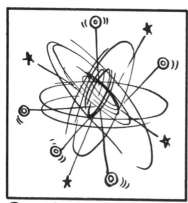

So they both go fast.

They say, "we have a mess."

Macadoo
photos a tall
bird,

a small bird,

and a

phony bird.

The boat will
not start.
Macadoo yanks
the cord.

Daisy wants to
yank the cord.
Macadoo says
no thanks.

Oh no!

Daisy sank
the boat.

This pen is out of ink.

Daisy shakes the pen.

She gets ink on the wall and

ink is in Macadoo's drink.

This bread is too hard to slice.

Hi-yah! Macadoo chops it.

The bread is sliced.

But the table is cracked.

Daisy sees an apple.

Daisy eats the apple.

Macadoo is mad.

The apple was his wax candle.

Sir, these glasses are cracked.

He fixes the glasses.

Look the glasses leak.

EIGHT

Teaching Math
OR
You're Not Going to
Chicken Out Now,
Are You?

When it comes to teaching their children math, a lot of mothers (and fathers) desert the ship or would like to. But don't you dare! If you skip out now you'll be denying your child some invaluable knowledge and developmental skills. Besides, with computers and calculators revolutionizing the job market and experts predicting that every well-equipped home will have an on-line computer by the year 2000 A.D., your child can't afford to be ignorant or afraid of numbers. After all, just because algebra 101 gave you migraines, there is no reason to pass this kind of legacy on to your child.[1]

So for the moment let's put aside any anxieties you may have, and instead talk about some of the differences and similarities between teaching math and reading, and how you can use each to make math as enjoyable as reading (and perhaps even easier to teach).

1. If the idea of teaching math or doing math incites fear in you, I recommend you read Sheila Tobias' book, *Overcoming Math Anxiety*. It explains why some of us are "math anxious" and provides a practical game plan for overcoming that fear.

MATH VS. READING

1. Math has fewer positive role models.

In my opinion the most significant differences between math and reading are the incidental lessons a child learns about each before he begins any formal classroom instruction.

For instance, before a child learns to read words he has already been exposed to a number of positive reading-related experiences through his parents and environment. He has been held close and been read to, had nursery rhymes recited to him, visited libraries, bookstores, and probably attended plays and puppet shows as well. Even when Mom or Dad comes home and grabs a newspaper or a book, the subtle message that reading is an important and worthwhile thing to do is being unconsciously relayed to the child.

On the other hand, look at a child's early math experiences. When he is very young and shows an interest in touching and playing with small objects, we discourage him with remarks such as "No, no, you might choke." Then we proceed to "child-proof" our homes and we put the buttons, beads, and the other manipulatable counting tools out of his reach—sometimes forever. As the child grows older and becomes more aware of numbers and of our using them, he sees us grumbling about an unbalanced checkbook or seething over an income tax form. Even when we hop on a scale we tend to grimace. While we're groaning, moaning, and complaining, the child is watching, learning, and developing an uncomfortable feeling about numbers.

The teaching implication, of course, is that if you want your child to be comfortable and competent in handling figures, you'll have to counter any negative forces that have been operating and find new ways to make math a more positive and enjoyable experience for both of you. If you've played the math-related games in Chapter Three, Thirty Days of Play,[2] you will

2. Math-related games include: Tin Can Alley (Game 3); Lotta-Lotto (Game 4); Restaurant (Game 8); Pickpocket Lady (Game 9); String Along (Game 10); Family Foot (Game 11); Color Coded (Game 20); One Box, Two Box (Game 26); Taste Test (Game 27).

have already set these wheels in motion. Later in this chapter we'll discuss additional ways to make math a more enjoyable and real experience for you and for your child.

2. Math is more predictable.

Another important way math differs from reading is that math tends to be a more predictable process. Once a child has mastered a basic math concept he can accurately apply that concept to almost every situation within his realm of experience. For example, in math the concept that one plus one equals two holds up whether you're talking about racing cars, jelly beans, or galaxies; whereas in reading, almost any concept you teach is loaded with "exceptions to." For instance, the symbol "a" can say: a as in air, a as in apple, a as in ate, a as in appear, etc.

The teaching implication is that the math concepts your child learns with you in class will probably translate more smoothly and without contraction into his everyday life outside of class than his early reading lessons did.

3. Math can be experienced.

One important way that math and reading are alike is that both can be experienced and acted out. In reading, a child can read a story and re-create the storyline through puppet shows, plays, or drawings. And with math, particularly the level you'll teach, your child can demonstrate almost any concept he learns through manipulatables such as bottle caps, buttons, or even his fingers.

The teaching implication is that your child will learn math concepts as concrete life experiences rather than as pencil and paper abstractions, and he can gain a basic understanding of our mathematical system that no workbook, textbook, or ditto sheet could ever provide.

Well, now are you willing to exorcise some of those math anxieties and realize that you don't need to be an Einstein to teach a child math? Okay—then let's get down to business.

LEARNING TO COUNT

A knowledge of the counting order of numbers is the basis of our mathematical system and is the primary factor in learning arithmetic. The child who knows how to count with meaning has already laid the groundwork for understanding addition, subtraction, multiplication, algebra, and the concept of equality.[3] In his book *Preventing Failure in the Primary Grades*, Siegfried Engelmann cites criteria for counting that children need to demonstrate they've acquired before they are taught addition, subtraction, and multiplication. They must be able to:

1. Count ten objects that are placed in a row and answer the question, "How many are there?"

2. Count from one given number to another within the 1–10 series, as in, "Please count from three to eight."

3. Indicate the number that comes after any number in the 1–10 series.

4. Predict the number of objects that will be in a group when one is added.

5. Identify the numerical symbols for the numbers one through ten.

Obviously, counting as defined by educators is more complicated than the "one, two, three . . ." recitation that many children do when they think they can count. To help your child learn counting as a thinking process rather than a meaningless

---

3. In the book *Teaching Disadvantaged Children in the Preschool* the authors say, "The several operations of arithmetic all refer to counting operations: the plus sign indicates counting ahead in the number order, the minus sign indicates counting backward, the times sign indicates counting by some number (e.g., counting every third number), and the equals sign refers to the end result of the counting operations, the number one ends up with."

jingle, let's first define some of the skills that lead to meaningful counting and then discuss ways you can help your child learn these skills at home.

Assignment #1. Developing Pre-Counting Skills

Educators have identified specific skills which lead to counting, which are:

classifying, comparing, ordering, matching, and recognizing patterns.

Of course, many children unconsciously develop these mathematical concepts through play and in their day-to-day interactions with others; however, there are many informal learning experiences that parents can provide to increase the likelihood that this will happen.

Your first assignment for this chapter is to read through the pre-counting skills section and practice some of the suggested activities with your child. Here is a breakdown of each sub-skill along with informal learning activities that help develop it:

CLASSIFYING

Classifying is the act of putting similar objects into the same group or set. Objects can be classified according to any number of attributes or characteristics such as:

1. physical properties—color, texture, composition, etc.;

2. category—toys, furniture, vehicles, plants, animals, etc.;

3. utility—things to ride in, cook with, write with, etc.;

4. or any combination of the above characteristics—animals you can ride on, toys that are made of wood, plants that are red, etc.

Suggested Related Indoor Activities:

- Let your child help you sort the wash into separate piles such as 1) dark clothes—light clothes, 2) laundry that is clothes—laundry that is not clothes, and 3) individual piles for each family member.
- Let your child get the mail and encourage him to sort it for you: letters go into one pile, magazines into another pile, and ads into yet another pile.
- After a visit to the supermarket let your child help you put away the groceries: canned products go in the cabinets, frozen foods go in the freezer, vegetables in the bin, etc.

Suggested Related Outdoor Activities

- Go on nature walks with your child and together pick a bunch of flowers, or collect interesting-looking rocks, or leaves, or whatever.
- Play the game "Category" where you think of a category and encourage your child to find examples of other things that fit into this category. For example, your category might be "vehicles." Things that belong in this category include cars, trucks, jeeps, etc.

Related Vocabulary:

You can help your child begin to develop the vocabulary he'll later need to describe more complex concepts if you start introducing some of these mathematical terms now. When you practice informal classifying activities with your child, occasionally substitute the word "set" for group, and the word "member" to describe the objects within a group. Encourage your child to also use these terms.

COMPARING

After similar objects are placed together in a group or set, it is quite natural to talk about the differences between them or to compare them. (This apple is bigger than that apple, this rock is heavier than that rock, etc.) Noticing the differences between similar objects helps a child fine-tune his discrimination skills, and sets the stage for an understanding of 1) quantity—this number is bigger than that number, and 2) standard measurement—he is two inches taller than I am.

Suggested Related Indoor Activities:
- When you pour milk into glasses, talk about whose glass has the least amount of milk.
- Compare portions or helpings of food, and talk about who eats the most, the next most, the least, etc.
- Keep track of your child's height through notches on a yardstick, wall chart, door, or tree, and over the course of a year talk about how much he has grown.

Suggested Related Outdoor Activities:
- Go on walks and talk about the differences between houses (some are one-story, others two-story, some are blue, others brown, etc.) or trees (some are tall, others shorter, some have berries, others don't, etc.)
- Talk about the weather; it was cold yesterday, but it is warmer today.
- Go on treasure hunts and find rocks, leaves, flowers, etc., and talk about the differences between them: 1) this rock is heavier than the other one, 2) this leaf is longer than that one, 3) this flower is more fragrant than that one, etc.

Related Vocabulary:
A lot of the vocabulary children need in order to talk about comparisons is learned in the natural course of conversation. However you can help your child develop the necessary vocabulary to talk intelligently about making comparisons if you share aloud and with your child the private thoughts that go into making a purchasing decision. For instance, if you are at the grocery store you can say something like "these carrots are bigger

than that bunch," "this loaf of bread feels softer than that other one," "a pound of bologna costs as much as a pound of steak," etc.

Try to work some of these words into your conversations:

bigger than	smaller than
less than	shorter than
equivalent to	fewer than
greater than	longer than
more than	as many as

ORDERING

Ordering is the process of arranging the members of a group or set in sequence according to specific characteristics or attributes. Children do a lot of ordering quite naturally in their play and perhaps you've noticed your child lining up wooden blocks, stuffed animals, or shoes, in a row according to size.

Suggested Related Indoor Activities:
- Pour milk into glasses and let your child line them up according to the fullest, the next fullest, and so on.
- Let your child line up pots and pans according to size.
- Encourage your child to put his stuffed animals (or some other toy group) in sequence from smallest to largest or vice versa.

Suggested Related Outdoor Activities:
- Go on a nature walk and find rocks, leaves, twigs, etc., and help your child arrange them according to size, weight, color, or whatever.

Related Vocabulary:
The vocabulary words for ordering are similar to those used in comparing. To that list add: "arrange" and "put in sequence."

MATCHING

Matching similar objects is one of the first steps toward understanding equality and inequality. Matching objects is often referred to as one-to-one correspondence. (One for me and one for you.)

Suggested Related Indoor Activities:
- Encourage your child to help you match socks, shoes, mittens, or anything that comes in pairs.
- Ask your child to help set the table and mention that each family member gets one plate, one cup, one fork, etc.
- When you help your child put on his clothes, say something like: one shoe for each foot, one sleeve for each arm, one hat for one head, etc.

Suggested Related Outdoor Activities:
- Go on nature walks and find two flowers, leaves, trees, etc., that look alike.
- While you're driving, call your child's attention to houses, cars, mail boxes, etc., that look alike. You could challenge him with a statement like: "Can you find other houses that look like this one?"

Related Vocabulary:
Most of the language you'll use in matching will come naturally in the course of conversation and no special words need to be introduced at this point.

RECOGNIZING PATTERNS

Recognizing patterns helps children see order and arrangement and helps prepare them for the predictability of our number system (two follows one, three follows two, four follows three, and so on.)

Suggested Related Indoor Activities:
- Talk about the patterns in the wallpaper, knitted sweaters, macrame hangings, and mention how the design repeats, alternates, or whatever.
- Provide your child with small manipulatables such as beads, macaroni noodles, blocks, pop bottle tops, etc., and encourage him to duplicate a pattern you've made or to make up a pattern of his own.

Suggested Related Outdoor Activities:
- Talk about the patterns in leaves, blades of grass, flowers.
- Point out the designs or patterns in landscaping. For instance, you might note that there are two rows of evergreens, or that all the trees are surrounded by rocks.

Related Vocabulary:

Most of the vocabulary you need in order to talk to your child about patterns will come naturally, but try to use words such as alternates, repeats, next, and row when you practice some of these activities with your child.

Assignment #2. Teaching Your Child to Count

The trick to teaching a child how to count with meaning is in gradually moving from the concreteness of manipulating physical objects to the abstractness of computing printed numbers. Unfortunately, this is usually learned in reverse—children learn numbers (1,2,3) without assigning them meaning (1 ball, two chairs, 3 cats).

Your second assignment for this chapter is to teach your child how to count. Use the criteria for counting on page 000 as eventual goals, but don't expect your child to reach this point immediately in his mathematical development.

Here is a sequence for teaching your child to count, along with some suggested activities:

1. Start with finger counting.
   - Touch and count the fingers on your child's hand (1,2,3,4,5 . . . five fingers).
   Touch and count the fingers on your hand (1,2,3,4,5 . . . five fingers).
   Encourage your child to count along with you.
   - Count up to the numbers between 1 and 5. Sometimes count four fingers, or two fingers, or one finger.

   Note: 1) Young children may lack the dexterity to count their own fingers and you may have to help them do that. 2) Some children may find memorizing five numbers at once too difficult, so teach only as many numbers at one time as your child can comfortably handle. Gradually build up to ten.

2. Move to counting small manipulatable objects such as poker chips, straws, pop bottle tops, blocks, etc.
   - Show your child how to touch and count out one through five objects.
   - Vary the number of chips you and your child count out. Sometimes count out two chips, four chips, or one chip.

3. Move to counting two-dimensional objects.
   - Draw lines (from one up to five) on the chalkboard and count them. Again, touch each line you count and encourage your child to do likewise.
   - Make flash cards with pictures of dots, fingers, balls, etc., and encourage your child to count the number of objects on each card. Vary the number sequence so that your child has to think about the counting process rather than just remember the order of the numbers. See Figure 22.

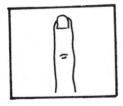 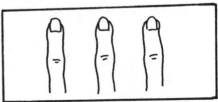

Figure 22

4. Introduce printed numbers.

- Use a number chart (or flash cards, or chalkboard) to teach your child numbers. Start with numbers 1 through 5 and gradually introduce the rest of the numbers on the chart. Remember to touch each number you say and to encourage your child to do likewise. See Figure 23.

1 2 3 4 5 6 7 8 9 10

Figure 23

- Point to numbers on the chart at random so that your child can learn to identify numbers out of sequence.
- Reinforce the numbers you've been teaching by reading counting books to your child:

The Berenstain Bears' Counting Book by Stanley and Janice Berenstain (Random House)
Ten Little Elephants by Robert Leydenfrost (Doubleday)
1, 2, 3, for the Library by Mary E. Little (Atheneum)
Fun on the Farm with Numbers by Barbara Loots (Hallmark)
Learn to Count by Richard Scarry (Golden Press)

5. Gradually add new numbers and more complex counting activities.

Assignment #3. Number Games

After you've introduced printed numbers to your child, you can play several games together that reinforce and build on his counting skills. Assignment #3 is to play number games with your child, and here are a few:

GAME 1   COUNTING PLATE

Section off a paper plate or cardboard circle into five divisions. Glue a varying number of beans, buttons, etc. to each section.

Give your child separate pieces of paper on which you have written the numbers 1, 2, 3, 4, and 5. Have your child match the appropriate number to the place on the plate having the corresponding number of objects. See Figure 24.

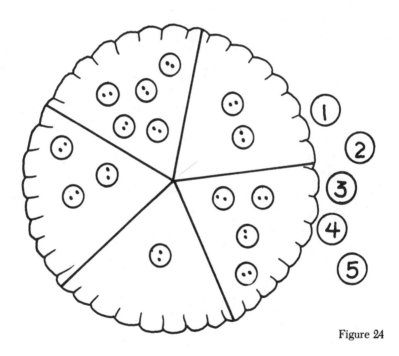

Figure 24

GAME 2   EGG CARTON COUNT

Place a few small objects in an egg carton. Ask your child to count and to touch the objects. Add a few more objects to the egg carton. Ask your child to count the total number of objects in the egg carton.

GAME 3   SHAKE, RATTLE, AND ROLL

Write the numbers 1 through 10 on the bottom of each cup in an egg carton. Place a small object such as a marble inside the carton. Close and shake the carton. Open the carton and have your child identify the number the marble lands on.

Variation: Instead of identifying the number the marble lands on, have your child give you the number that comes after it. For instance, if the marble lands on "3," ask your child to tell you what number comes after three (four).

GAME 4   NUMBER SPINNER

Fasten a cardboard arrow to the center of a cardboard circle. Use a paper fastener or screw and nut. Write numbers your child has learned around the outer edges of the cardboard circle. Show your child how to turn the spinner and have him identify the number the arrow points at.

Variation: Give your child a pile of small counters (buttons, beads, blocks) and have him count out the number of objects that the arrow indicates; e.g., if the arrow points to "5," he should count out five objects. See Figure 25.

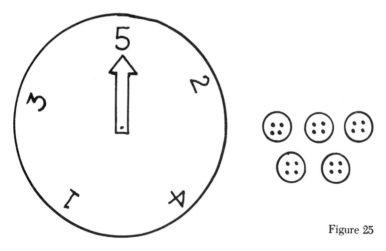

Figure 25

GAME 5   WORD PROBLEMS

Use simple word problems to help your child perform simple math operations in his head.

> *Examples:* If there are two birds in the tree and one more bird came, then how many birds are now in the tree?
>
> If we have four cookies on a plate and Sara ate two cookies, how many cookies are left?

Assignment #4. Build on the Counting Sub-Skills

Now that your child has learned the concept of number, you can tie in numbers with some of the informal learning activities you practice together. Here are a few examples of how to do it:

Classifying—Count the number of objects in a set.

Comparing—Talk about height, weight, etc., in terms of numbers: e.g., you weighed two pounds more today than you weighed a month ago, you are two inches taller now than you were last year, etc.

Ordering—Put a varying number of dots (circles, balls) on separate paper plates and have your child put them in sequence, from the plate with the most dots to the plate with the fewest dots.

Matching—Introduce the equal sign ("=") and explain to your child that as many objects as he puts on one side of the equal sign, he must put on the other side of the equal sign. Demonstrate the concept with small counters.

Recognizing Patterns—Make a number line and count every other number. Help your child count by two's and three's. See Figure 26.

Assignment #4 is to use numbers in learning activities that you play with your child.

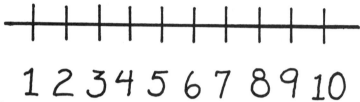

Figure 26

SUMMARY OF ASSIGNMENTS FOR CHAPTER EIGHT

1. Practice pre-counting activities with your child.

2. Teach your child how to count.

3. Play number games with your child.

4. Use numbers in learning activities that you play with your child.

APPENDIX 1
FURTHER READING,
REFERENCE

Child-Parent Relationships

Reference Books

How to Parent. Fitzhugh Dodson, New American Library (NAL).

On Becoming a Family. T. Berry Brazelton, Delacorte.

P.E.T. (Parent Effectiveness Training). Thomas Gordon, McKay.

Newsletters and Magazines

The Center for Parents Newsletter
Education Institute
55 Chapel St.
Newton, MA 02160

Gifted Children Monthly
P.O. Box 115
Sewell, NJ 08080

Growing Child Research Review
Dunn and Hargitt, Inc.
P.O. Box 620
Lafayette, IN 47902

Learning
P.O. Box 2580
Boulder, CO 80322

Nurturing News
187 Caselli Ave.
San Francisco, CA 94114

Parent's Magazine
685 Third Ave.
New York, NY 10019

Totline
Warren Publishing House, Inc.
P.O. Box 2255
Everett, WA 98203

Booklets, Pamphlets, Brochures
Becoming a Nation of Readers: What Parents Can Do
Consumer Information Center
Pueblo, CO 81009
To order, send $.50 for each copy to the above address.

Organizations

American Library Association
50 East Huron, Chicago, IL 60611
Phone: (800) 545-2433
Web site: www.ala.org/

The Council for Exceptional Children
1920 Association Drive, Reston, VA 20191-1589
Phone: (888) CEC-SPED
Web site: www.cec.sped.org/

International Childbirth Education Association, Inc.
P.O. Box 20048, Minneapolis, MN 55420
Phone: (612) 854-8660
Web site: www.icea.org/

International Reading Association
800 Barksdale Road, P.O. Box 8139
Newark, DE 19714-8139
Phone: (302) 731-1600
Web site: www.reading.org/

La Leche League International
1400 N. Meacham Rd, Schaumburg, IL 60173-4048
Phone: (847) 519-7730
Web site: www.lalecheleague.org/

Learning Disabilities Association
4156 Library Road, Pittsburgh, PA 15234-1349
Phone: (412) 341-1515
Web site: www.1danatl.org/

National Association for the Education of Young Children
1509 16th Street NW, Washington, DC 20036
Phone: (800) 424-2460
Web site: www.naeyc.org/

National Association for Gifted Children
1707 L Street NW, Suite 550, Washington, DC 20036
Phone: (202) 785-4268
Web site: www.nagc.org/

National Black Child Development Institute
1023 15th Street NW, Suite 600, Washington, DC 20005
Phone: (202) 387.1281
Web site: www.nbcdi.org/

National Council of Teachers of English
1111 Kenyon Rd., Urbana, IL 61801
Phone: (800) 369-6283
Web site: www.ncte.org/

National Council of Teachers of Mathematics
1906 Association Drive, Reston, VA 20191
Phone: (703) 620-9840
Web site: www.nctm.org/

National Education Association
1201 16th Street NW, Washington, DC 20036
Phone: (202) 833-4000
Web site: www.nea.org/

National PTA
330 North Wabash Ave., Suite 2100, Chicago, IL 60611
Phone: (800) 307-4782
Web site: www.pta.org/

Parents Without Partners
1650 South Dixie Highway, Suite 510, Boca Raton, FL 33432
Phone: (561) 391-8833
Web site: www.parentswithoutpartners.org/

Web sites

ERIC Clearinghouse on Elementary and Early Childhood Education
www.ericeece.org/

Homeschooling Information and Resources Pages
www.home-ed-magazine.com

Homeschooling Today
www.homeschooltoday.com

National Institutes of Health
www.nih.gov/health

Parent Soup
www.parentsoup.com/

Practical Homeschooling
www.home-school.com

Softchalk Learning Systems, Inc.
www.softchalklearning.com

U.S. Department of Education
www.ed.gov/

General Books

Anderson, Richard, and the Commission on Reading. *Becoming a Nation of Readers*. National Council of Teachers of English.

Bennett, T., B. Lingerfelt, and Nelson. *Developing Individualized Family Support Plans: A Training Manual*. Brookline Books.

Segal, Marilyn and Wendy Masi. *Your Child at Play: Five to Eight Years*. Newmarket Press.

Segal, Marilyn and Wendy Masi. *Your Child at Play: Three to Five Years*. Newmarket Press.

Snow, Catherine E., M. Susan Burns, and Peg Griffin, eds. *Preventing Reading Difficulties*. The National Academy of Sciences.

Teaching Reading and Language Skills

Books and Programs

Becoming a Nation of Readers. Center for the Study of Reading, University of Illinois, Champaign, IL.

Learning Through Play. Jean Marzollo and Janice Lloyd, Harper & Row.

A Parent's Guide to Children's Reading. Nancy Larrick, Westminster.

The Read-Aloud Handbook. Jim Trelease, Penguin.

Booklets, Pamphlets, Brochures

10 Ways to Help Your Children Become Better Readers. The Center for the Study of Reading, University of Illinois, Champaign, IL.

Organizations

American Library Association
Public Information Office
50 East Huron St.
Chicago, IL 60611
Publishes several booklets on helping children read at home.
   Write for list.

American Montessori
150 Fifth Ave.
New York, NY 10011

Center for the Study of Reading
University of Illinois
Champaign, IL 61820
Publishes a number of books and brochures on how to improve
   reading.

International Reading Association
P.O. Box 8139
Newark, DE 19711
Publishes several pamphlets to help your child learn to read
   better.

National Association for Education of Young Children
1834 Connecticut Ave. NW
Washington, DC 20009

National Council of the Teachers of English
1111 Kenyon Rd.
Urbana, IL 61801
Publishes books, booklets, etc., on teaching children reading
and language skills.

Reading Reform Foundation
Suite 436
949 Market St.
Tacoma, WA 98402
Publishes newsletters, reference book lists, and other infor-
mation on teaching phonics.

APPENDIX 2
ADDITIONAL TERMS

Consonant blends. Two or three consonant combinations that are read by sliding the sounds together in sequence. Examples: bl (blue), cl (cloud), pr (pride), tr (tree), tw (twin), spl (splash), str (street)

Murmur diphthongs. Another name for r-controlled letters (h*er*, *car*, s*ir*, t*urn*)

Schwa sound. The short u sound as represented by the symbol ə. Any vowel can have a schwa sound and here are a few examples: appear (ə - pir) polite (p ə - lit)

APPENDIX 3
GAME REFERENCES

I've tried to detail to the best of my knowledge the origin of the games in Chapter Three. One book that is cited frequently is *School Before Six*. This book is a comprehensive two-volume text on teaching young children through games and activities. Many of the games I found in *School Before Six* were games I had used, played, or thought of before I ever read the book. However, if the idea for a game I used did originate or appear in *School Before Six*, I do mention that.

1. Ouchless Obstacle Course. Variation of games in *School Before Six* by Hodgden, *Teaching Reading* by Walcutt.

2. Follow-the-Arrow. I made this game up at home, although a similar approach to left-right tracking is used in *DISTAR Reading Program* by Engelmann.

3. Tin Can Alley. My son made this game up although there are many variations of this one floating around.

4. Lotta-Lotto. This game is very common and is widely used in preschools and nursery schools. Commercial lotto games can also be purchased. However, the game was mentioned in *School Before Six* by Hodgden, *Teaching Montessori in the Preschool Years* by Hainstock.

5. Sound Zoo. Original, as far as I know.

6. Biscuit Bake. Paraphrased from *Thinking Is Child's Play* by Sharp.

7. Storytime. No reference required.

8. Restaurant. This is a common activity in nursery schools and kindergarten and it is usually taught as a lotto game. A similar game is mentioned in *School Before Six* by Hodgden.

9. Pickpocket Lady. This game is original as far as I know, but the idea of using a bag or box to "feel" textures or describe objects is a common early education activity.

10. String Along. This is a standard in Montessori programs. Other sources with the same idea are *Child Learning Through Child Play* by Gordon, *Teaching Montessori in the Preschool Years* by Hainstock, *School Before Six* by Hodgden.

11. Family Foot. Tracing and comparing parts of the child's body—hands, feet, head, etc., is a common early childhood education activity. However a similar tracing game can be found in *Thinking Is Child's Play* by Sharp.

12. Egg Carton Switch. Again, here is yet another commonly played activity that we played before I read about similar games in *School Before Six* by Hodgden, *Teaching Reading* by Walcutt.

13. Stacia's Synonym Match. This idea came from my sister-in-law who works at a nursery school in Minneapolis.

14. Lids and Bottles. This is a common activity in preschools and nursery schools and it is mentioned in *School Before Six* by Hodgden.

15. Chalkboard Jungle. This was not a previous idea of mine, (although I have similar ideas) and this game is paraphrased from one I read in *School Before Six* by Hodgden.

16. Emergency. Of course parents always ask their children how they would respond should an emergency arise and a similar game can be found in *The Complete Book of Children's Play* by Hartley.

17. Picture Talk. Original as far as I know.

18. I'm the Boss. This is a common early childhood education idea, and other books where I've seen similar games include *Teaching Reading* by Walcutt, *The Complete Book of Children's Play* by Hartley, *School Before Six* by Hodgden, *Sesame Street* TV Program.

19. Rhyme-Time. This game is paraphrased from *School Before Six* by Hodgden.

20. Color Coded. Matching color cards is a common way to teach a child his or her colors. The same approach is used in *Learning Through Play* by Marzollo and Lloyd.

21. Ann's Antonym Match Game. This idea came from my sister-in-law.

22. Word Painting. This is a variation of a similar game with the same title found in *Games to Improve Your Child's English* by Hurwitz.

23. Painless Puzzles. I saw this idea on *Captain Kangaroo* and a similar activity appears in *School Before Six* by Hodgden.

24. Preposition Position. I learned this method of teaching prepositions while in undergraduate school from *DISTAR Language Program* by Engelmann.

25. Tongue Twister. I got this idea from a speech therapist in Normal, Illinois.

26. One Box, Two Box. The idea came from *Let's Play Math* by Holt and Dienes.

27. Taste Test. This activity is common in nursery schools, and similar ideas can be found in *School Before Six* by Hodgden, *Teaching Montessori in the Preschool Years* by Hainstock. (My son's kindergarten teacher also uses this idea in her classroom.)

28. Finger Puppets. The use of various kinds of puppets is common in early childhood education and here are other sources with similar ideas on finger puppets: *Potpourri of Puppetry* by Bates, *Finger Puppets* by Ross, *School Before Six* by Hodgden.

29. Popsicle Stick Puppet. Other sources: *Potpourri of Puppetry* by Bates, *School Before Six* by Hodgden.

30. Sock Puppet. Other sources: *Potpourri of Puppetry* by Bates, *School Before Six* by Hodgden.

A few of the games in Chapter Four are variations of games I learned from Siegfried Engelmann, and they also appear in Douglas Carnine's book *Direct Instruction Reading*. (Doug is a former student of Engelmann's, so our approach to teaching reading is quite similar. However, his book is designed for teachers while mine is designed for mothers.) The games which overlap somewhat are:

1. Word Division (approach used by Carnine and Engelmann)

2. Slow Poke (approach used by Carnine and Engelmann)

3. Rhymes with It (Carnine and Engelmann)

BIBLIOGRAPHY

Ainsworth, M. *Patterns of Attachment*. Halsted Press, 1979.

Aukerman, R. C. *Approaches to Beginning Reading*. Wiley, 1971.

Axline, V. *Play Therapy*. Houghton Mifflin, 1976.

Baratta-Lorton, M. *Workjobs for Parents*. Addison-Wesley, 1975.

Bates, E. and Lowes, R. *Potpourri of Puppetry*. Fearon, 1976.

Beck, J. *How to Raise a Brighter Child*. Pocket Books, 1975.

Becker, W. *Parents Are Teachers: A Child Management Program*. Research Press, 1971.

Bereiter, C. and Englemann, S. *Teaching Disadvantaged Children in the Preschool*. Prentice-Hall, 1966.

Bettelheim, B. *Dialogues With Mothers*. Avon, 1971.

Bettelheim, B. *The Uses of Enchantment*. Random House, 1976.

Blumenfeld, S. L. *The New Illiterates*. Arlington Press, 1972.

Boston Women's Health Book Collective. *Ourselves and Our Children*. Random House, 1978.

Carew, J. "Black Beginnings: A Longitudinal Videotaped Observational Study of the Rearing and Development of Infants in Black Families." *Parenthood in a Changing Society*. ERIC Clearinghouse on Elementary and Early Childhood Education, 1979, p. 26–48.

Carnine, D. *Direct Instruction Reading*. Merrill, 1979.

Chall, J. *Learning to Read, the Great Debate*. McGraw-Hill, 1967.

Copeland, R. W. *Math Activities for Children.* Merrill, 1979.

Diehl, K. *Johnny Still Can't Read—But You Can Teach Him at Home.* Johnny, Inc., 1977.

Dobson, J. *Dare to Discipline.* Bantam, 1977.

Dodson, F. *How to Parent.* NAL, 1973.

Dodson, F. *How to Discipline With Love.* NAL, 1978.

Durkin, D. *Children Who Read Early.* Teachers College Press, 1966.

Durkin, D. *Phonics and the Teaching of Reading.* Teachers College Press, 1962.

Durkin, D. *Teaching Them to Read.* Allyn-Bacon, 1978.

Durkin, D. *Teaching Young Children to Read.* Allyn-Bacon, 1980.

Emery, D. *Teach Your Preschooler to Read.* Simon & Schuster, 1975.

Engelmann, S. *Preventing Failure in the Primary Grades.* Science Research Associates, 1969.

Engelmann, S. and T. *Give Your Child A Superior Mind.* Cornerstone, 1981.

Flesch, R. *Why Johnny Can't Read.* Harper & Row, 1966.

Flesch, R. *Why Johnny Still Can't Read.* Harper & Row, 1981.

Foltzer, M. *Professor Phonics Gives Sound Advice.* St. Ursula Academy, 1974.

Fraiberg, S. *Every Child's Birthright: In Defense of Mothering.* Basic Books, 1977.

Ginott, H. *Between Parent and Child.* Avon, 1973.

Gordon, I. *Child Learning Through Child Play.* St. Martins, 1972.

Gordon, T. *Parent Effectiveness Training.* NAL, 1975.

Gordon, T. *P.E.T. in Action.* Wyden, 1976.

Hainstock, E. *The Essential Montessori.* NAL, 1978.

Hainstock, E. *Teaching Montessori in the Preschool Years.* NAL, 1978.

Hartley, R. and Golderson, R. *The Complete Book of Children's Play.* Thomas Cromwell, 1970.

Hearne, B. *Choosing Books for Children: A Commonsense Guide.* Delacorte, 1981.

Hodgden, L., Koetter, J., and others. *School Before Six: A Diagnostic Approach,* Volumes I and II, CEMREL, 1974.

Holt, J. *How Children Learn*. Dell, 1970.

Holt, J. *Teach Your Own*. Delacorte, 1981.

Holt, M. and Dienes, Z. *Let's Play Math*. Walker, 1973.

Hunt, J. McV. *Intelligence and Experience*. Ronald Press, 1961.

Hurwitz, A. B. and Goddard, A. *Games to Improve Your Child's English*. Fireside, 1969.

Jones, S. *Learning for Little Kids*. Houghton Mifflin, 1979.

Karnes, M. and others. *Nurturing Academic Talent in Early Education: Math*. Bureau of Education for the Handicapped, Washington, D.C., March 1979.

Katz, L. "Contemporary Perspectives on the Roles of Mothers." *Parenthood in a Changing Society*, 1979, pp. 8–26.

Katz, L. *Helping Others Learn to Teach*. ERIC, 1979.

Kohl, H. *Growing With Your Children*. Little, Brown, 1978.

Kusnetz, L. *Your Child Can Be A Super Reader*. Learning House, 1980.

Lamme, L., Cox, V. and others. *Raising Readers*. The National Council of Teachers of English, 1980.

Larrick, N. *A Parent's Guide to Children's Reading*. Doubleday, 1975.

Levenstein, P. "Cognitive Growth in Preschoolers through Verbal Interaction with Mothers." *American Journal of Orthopsychiatry*, 1970, *40*, pp. 426–432.

Levenstein, P. "Symposium on Parent-Centered Education: 2. Learning through (and from) Mothers." *Childhood Education*, 1971, *48*, pp. 130–134.

Liedtke, W. "Rational Counting." *Arithmetic Teacher*, October 1978, pp. 20–26.

Lockhart, C. F. *Discover Intensive Phonics for Yourself*. Char-L Publications, 1980.

Maffel, A., and Buckley, P. *Teaching Preschool Math*. Human Sciences Press, 1980.

Marzollo, J. *Learning Through Play*. Harper & Row, 1972.

Matthias, M. "Counting Books: The Children's Choice." *Teacher*, February 1980, *197*, pp. 103–104.

McEathron, M. *Your Child Can Learn to Read*. Grosset & Dunlap, 1952.

McQueen, P. *Developing Potential Reading Ability*. McQueen Publ. Co., 1965.

Morgan, M. *Total Woman*. Revell, 1973.

Orton, J. L. *A Guide to Teaching Phonics*. The Orton Reading Center, 1976.

Payne, J. N., Editor. *Mathematics Learning in Early Childhood*. National Council of Teachers of Mathematics, 1975.

Piaget, J. "How Children Form Mathematical Concepts." *Scientific American*, November 1953.

Rogers, C. *Client-Centered Therapy*. Houghton Mifflin, 1951.

Ross, L. *Finger Puppets*. Lothrop, Lee and Shepard, 1971.

Ross, L. *Hand Puppets*. Lothrop, Lee and Shepard, 1969.

Sharp, E. *Thinking Is Child's Play*. Dutton, 1969.

Silcox, D. *Woman Time: Personal Time Management for Women Only!* Wyden Books, 1980.

Sparkman, B. and Carmichael, A. *Blueprint for a Brighter Child*. McGraw-Hill, 1973.

Spodek, B. *Early Childhood Education*. Prentice-Hall, 1973.

Tobias, S. *Overcoming Math Anxiety*. W. W. Norton, 1978.

Chicago Tribune. *Shortcuts to Reading Series*, 1964.

Walcutt, C. and others. *Teaching Reading*. Macmillan, 1974.

Weikart, D. "Parent Involvement through Home Teaching." *High Scope Research Foundation Report*, 1974-75.

Weiss, H. and M. *Home is a Learning Place*. Little, Brown, 1976.

White, B., Kaban, B. T., and others. *The Origins of Human Competence: The Final Report of the Harvard Preschool Project*. Lexington Books, 1979.

Zaslavsky, C. "An Early Start in Math." *Teacher*, November-December 1979, pp. 123-124.

Index

About the Author

Teresa Savage is an Associate Dean at the College of Communications, University of Illinois-Urbana. She has served as a project consultant to Walt Disney's Buena Vista Home Video, the U.S. Standards on English/Language Arts, and Head Start. A former teacher, she is a published poet and fiction writer. She co-founded Softchalk Learning Systems, Inc., (www.softchalklearning.com), a technology company devoted to the education of young children. She has two children whom she taught to read and count at home as preschoolers. Teresa Savage lives in Urbana, Illinois.

Childcare/Parenting Books from Newmarket Press

DR. MARILYN SEGAL'S YOUR CHILD AT PLAY SERIES
In Five Volumes, From Birth to Eight Years
New Second Edition completely revised and updated
With more than 700 Photographs,
Foreword by Wendy Masi, Ph.D.

Established in 1986, this now updated and expanded series, based on more than twenty years of research and observation, is written in jargon-free, parent-friendly language. These books respect cultural differences and recognize the value of different parenting styles. Their focus is to help parents and caregivers turn everyday routines into playful learning opportunities and enhance communication between children and adults. The photos of real children at play are candid and reflect all cultures.

"These terrific books are handsome, engaging, and chock full of practical knowledge about child care and guidance—what's more, they provide numerous ways for parents and children to have fun as they explore each other's worlds."—*Edward Zigler, Sterling Professor of Psychology, Yale University*

YOUR CHILD AT PLAY: BIRTH TO ONE YEAR
Discovering the Senses and Learning about the World
352 pp. 7¼" x 9". 183 photographs. Bibliography. Index.
1-55704-334-5. $27.95. Hardcover. 1-55704-330-2. $17.95. Paperback.

YOUR CHILD AT PLAY: ONE TO TWO YEARS
Exploring, Learning, Making Friends, and Pretending
304 pp. 7¼" x 9". 242 photographs. Bibliography. Index.
1-55704-335-3. $27.95. Hardcover. 1-55704-331-0. $16.95. Paperback.

YOUR CHILD AT PLAY: TWO TO THREE YEARS
Growing Up, Language, and the Imagination
240 pp. 7¼" x 9". 132 photographs. Bibliography. Index.
1-55704-336-1. $27.95. Hardcover. 1-55704-332-9. $16.95. Paperback.

YOUR CHILD AT PLAY: THREE TO FIVE YEARS
Conversation, Creativity, and Learning Letters, Words and Numbers
304 pp. 7¼" x 9". 120 photographs. Bibliography. Index.
1-55704-337-X. $27.95. Hardcover. 1-55704-333-7. $16.95. Paperback.

YOUR CHILD AT PLAY: FIVE TO EIGHT YEARS
Building Friendships, Expanding Interests, and Resolving Conflicts
256 pp. 7¼" x 9". 89 photographs. Bibliography, Index.
1-55704-402-3. $27.95. Hardcover. 1-55704-401-5. $17.95. Paperback.

IN TIME AND WITH LOVE
Caring for the Special Needs Infant and Toddler—Second Edition
Marilyn Segal, Ph.D. with Roni Leiderman, Ph.D. Foreword by Wendy Masi Ph.D.

In a format similar to the acclaimed *Your Child At Play* series, illustrated with over 100 photos, and based on the latest research, this new edition gives parents of preterm and handicapped children from birth to preteen sensitive, practical advice on care and activities to enhance development.

208 pages. 7" x 9". Bibliography, Resources, Index, Illustrations.
1-55704-445-7. $17.95. Paperback. 1-55704-454-6. $29.95. Hardcover.

THE WHAT'S HAPPENING TO MY BODY? BOOK FOR BOYS

A Growing-Up Guide for Parents and Sons, Third Edition
Lynda Madaras with Area Madaras, Foreword by Martin Anderson, M.D.

Selected as a "Best Book for Young Adults" by the American Library Association, this classic puberty education book for 8- to 15-year-old boys (over 500,000 copies sold) is now thoroughly updated and freshly redesigned for the first time in 12 years. This classic book covers the body's changing size and shape, hair, voice changes, perspiration, pimples, the reproductive organs, sexuality, puberty in girls and adds new sections on diet, exercise, and health. It also includes vital information on AIDS, STDs, and birth control appropriate for this age group, and an introduction for parents and educators.

272 pages. 5¼" x 8". 48 black-and-white drawings. Bibliography, Index, Resources.
1-55704-443-0. $12.95. Paperback. 1-55704-447-3. $22.95. Hardcover.

THE WHAT'S HAPPENING TO MY BODY? BOOK FOR GIRLS

A Growing-Up Guide for Parents and Daughters, Third Edition
Lynda Madaras with Area Madaras Foreword by Marcia Herman-Giddens, PA, Dr. PH

Selected as a "Best Book for Young Adults" by the American Library Association, the classic puberty education book for 8- to 15-year-old girls (over 500,000 copies sold) is now thoroughly updated and freshly redesigned for the first time in 12 years. Now for the first time since the medical journal *Pediatrics* published its news-making, large-scale study indicating that puberty begins in girls even earlier than previously believed, Lynda Madaras has thoroughly rewritten, updated, and expanded her classic book to address the younger girl and her concerns.

304 pages. 5¼" x 8". 51 black-and-white drawings. Bibliography, Index, Resources.
1-55704-444-9. $12.95. Paperback. 1-55704-448-1. $22.95. Hardcover.

MY BODY, MY SELF FOR GIRLS

A What's Happening to My Body? Quizbook
Lynda Madaras & Area Madaras

In the million-copy *What's Happening to My Body?* series for preteens and teens (8- to 15-year-olds), in a fresh new edition (previously sold over 90,000 copies), this fact-filled and fun-filled journal/activity book has been expanded to include more letters from kids, answers the questions girls ages 8 to 15 have about growing up. Illustrated with drawings, cartoons, and photos, here are stories, quizzes, exercises, checklists, suggestions for diary keeping, illustrations, and lots of personal anecdotes about physical changes and the different feelings girls have about them. Everything affected by the onset of puberty is covered, from body image, diet, height, weight, pimples, and cramps, to first periods, first bras, and first impressions.

128 pages. 7¼" x 9". Over 40 drawings. 1-55704-441-4. $12.95. Paperback.

MY BODY, MY SELF FOR BOYS

A What's Happening to My Body? Quizbook
Lynda Madaras & Area Madaras

With more than 65,000 copies sold, this journal/activity book was inspired by thousands of letters from boys all over the world, encouraging them to address their concerns head-on. Illustrated with drawings, cartoons, and photos, here are stories, quizzes, exercises, checklists, suggestions for diary keeping, illustrations, and lots of personal anecdotes about physical changes and the different feelings boys have about them.

112 pages. 7¼" x 9". Over 60 drawings. 1-55704-440-6. $12.95. Paperback.

MY FEELINGS, MY SELF
A Growing-Up Guide for Girls—Second Edition
Lynda Madaras & Area Madaras

A complement to *My Body, My Self for Girls*, this book for preteens, teens, parents, and educators focuses on relationships, feelings, self-knowledge, problem-solving with parents, handling peer pressure, and making friends. Filled with quizzes, exercises, letters, and personal stories from readers and students. Over 60,000 copies sold. "Another winner from Madaras . . . Here's hard to find information, instructions for naming feelings, sending and receiving messages, and using problem-solving techniques."—*Publishers Weekly*

160 pages. 7¼" x 9". 30 drawings, bibliography. 1-55704-442-2. $12.95. Paperback.

BEYOND THE BIG TALK
Every Parent's Guide to Raising Sexually Healthy Teens—From Middle School to College
By Debra Haffner, M.P.H.

Debra Haffner's new book, picks up from where her first, award-winning book, *From Diapers to Dating*, left off. Delivers Haffner's values-oriented approach to raising sexually healthy teenagers in her highly praised direct and informative style.

240 pp. 6" x 9". Bibliography, index. 1-55704-472-4. $23.95. Hardcover.

FROM DIAPERS TO DATING
A Parent's Guide to Raising Sexually Healthy Children
By Debra W. Haffner, M.P.H.

Approved by Parents' Choice 1999, praised in *Time*, *Newsweek*, and *Library Journal*—first time in paperback for this exceptional book—a leading sexuality educator's warm, practical, step-by-step program for helping parents provide accurate information and communicate their own values to their children.

"Realistic, practical, and informative—the best kind of guide for being a better parent."—*Kirkus Reviews*

240 pp. 6" x 9". Bibliography, index.
1-55704-426-0. $14.95. Paperback. 1-55704-385-X. $23.95. Hardcover.

KEEP YOUR KIDS TOBACCO-FREE
Smart Strategies for Parents of Children Ages 3 Through 19
By Robert Schwebel, Ph.D.

This easy-to-read, invaluable book offers parents a powerful program for preventing or ending their children's tobacco addiction.

"This book contains the best information I've seen to help parents stop the addiction before it starts."—Andrew Weil, M.D.

288 pp. 5 3/8" x 8". Index. 1-55704-369-8. $14.95. Paperback.

SAYING NO IS NOT ENOUGH
Helping Your Kids Make Wise Decisions About Alcohol, Tobacco, and Other Drugs—A Guide for Parents of Children Ages 3 Through 19
By Robert Schwebel, Ph.D. Introduction by Benjamin Spock, M.D.

A Parents' Choice Award-winner ... one of the nation's leading family therapists and substance abuse prevention experts presents a complete, step-by-step program, time-tested over the last 25 years.

304 pp. 5¼" x 8". Bibliography. Index. 1-55704-318-3. $14.95. Paperback.

HOW DO WE TELL THE CHILDREN?
A Step-by-Step Guide for Helping Children Two to Teen Cope When Someone Dies—Updated Edition
By Dan Schaefer and Christine Lyons, Foreword by David Peretz, M.D.

This compassionate, step-by-step guide to talking about death with children is updated with new material on AIDS, the loss of a companion animal, and talking with the mentally handicapped.

208 pp. 5¼" x 8¼". Bibliography. Index.
1-55704-430-9. $24.95. Hardcover. 1-55704-425-2. $14.95. Paperback.

RAISING YOUR JEWISH/CHRISTIAN CHILD
How Interfaith Parents Can Give Children the Best of Both Their Heritages—Second Edition
By Lee F. Gruzen

Based on hundreds of interviews, extensive research and personal experience, this new and updated version of the book offers a wealth of insight into the complicated feelings and loyalties that parents, children, grandparents, and clergy bring to this subject.

"A thoughtful and pioneering guide for the perplexed parent."—*Library Journal*

288 pages. 5" x 8". Bibliography. Index. 1-55704-414-7. $16.95. Paperback.

HOW TO HELP YOUR CHILD OVERCOME YOUR DIVORCE
By Elissa P. Benedek, M.D., and Catherine F. Brown

This invaluable manual by one of the nation's top experts guides parents facing the upheaval of divorce in helping their children adjust to separation and divorce; avoiding many of the parenting pitfalls common after divorce; keeping the relationship between ex-spouses as free of conflict as possible; and more.

"*How to Help Your Child Overcome Divorce* is a major contribution to parents who are facing the personal upheaval of divorce."—Lawrence A. Stone, M.D. President, American Academy of Child & Adolescent Psychiatry

336 pp. 6" x 9". Resources, Index. 1-55704-461-9. $15.95. Paperback.

BABY MASSAGE
Parent-Child Bonding Through Touch—Revised Edition
By Amelia D. Auckett, Introduction by Dr. Tiffany Field

With over 40,000 copies sold, this classic handbook on baby massage presents a fully illustrated, time-tested approach to the techniques and benefits of parent-child touch, including the process of bonding and body contact, baby massage as an alternative to drugs, and baby massage as an expression of love.

128 pp. 5¼" x 8¼". 34 photos & drawings. Bibliography. Index. 1-55704-022-2. $11.95. Paperback.

LOVING HANDS
The Traditional Art of Baby Massage
By Frederick Leboyer, M.D.

Now in paperback, the ancient art of baby massage is described in depth by renowned obstetrician Frederick Leboyer, illustrated with his own photographs. He uses his deep insight into childcare—as well as knowledge gleaned from traveling in India—to show us how, in the weeks and months following birth, we can use the flowing rhythms of the art of baby massage to communicate our love and strength to our infants.

144 pp. 8" x 10 7/8". 70 black-and-white photos. 1-55704-314-0. $16.95. Paperback.

MOTHERING THE NEW MOTHER
Women's Feelings & Needs After Childbirth: A Support & Resource Guide—Revised and Updated Edition
By Sally Placksin

For the expectant and new mom, this acclaimed all-in-one support guide includes resources, networks, information, stories, and advice provided by doctors, nurses, midwives, new mothers, and other caregivers.

"Thoroughly well-written and very much needed."—*Booklist*

420 pp. 6" x 9". Resources. Bibliography. Index. 1-55704-317-5. $18.95. Paperback.

INNER BEAUTY, INNER LIGHT
Yoga for Pregnant Women
By Frederick Leboyer, M.D., Introduction by B.K.S. Iyengar

In matchless prose and stunning photographs, Frederick Leboyer discusses the importance and beauty of yoga for pregnant women. He shows how they can use yoga to move toward healthy and joyous childbearing, and how the health benefits will far outlast the birthing process—for both mother and child.

256 pp. 8" x 10 7/8". 100 black-and-white photos. 1-55704-315-9. $18.95. Paperback.

Books are available at your local bookstore, or use this coupon. Enclose a check or money order payable to Newmarket Press and send to:

Newmarket Press, 18 East 48th Street, New York, NY, 10017
Tel. (212) 832-3575, (800) 669-3903, Fax (212) 832-3629, E-mail: mailbox@newmarketpress.com

Childcare/Parenting Books from Newmarket Press

Name _____

Affiliation _____

Address _____

City _____ State _____

Zip _____ Telephone # _____

Email _____

ISBN	Qty.	Title, Author	Price	Amt.
1-55704-022-2	____	Baby Massage, Auckett	$11.95pb	____
1-55704-472-4	____	Beyond the Big Talk, Haffner	23.95hc	____
1-55704-385-X	____	From Diapers to Dating, Haffner	23.95hc	____
1-55704-426-0	____	From Diapers to Dating, Haffner	14.95pb	____
1-55704-425-2	____	How Do We Tell the Children?, Schaefer	14.95pb	____
1-55704-430-9	____	How Do We Tell the Children?, Schaefer	24.95hc	____
1-55704-461-9	____	How to Help…Divorce, Benedek/Brown	15.95pb	____
1-55704-369-8	____	Keep Your Kids Tobacco-Free, Schwebel	14.95pb	____
1-55704-445-7	____	In Time and With Love, Segal	17.95pb	____
1-55704-454-6	____	In Time and With Love, Segal	29.95hc	____
1-55704-315-9	____	Inner Beauty, Inner Light, Leboyer	18.95pb	____
1-55704-314-0	____	Loving Hands, Leboyer	16.95pb	____
1-55704-317-5	____	Mothering the New Mother, Placksin	18.95pb	____
1-55704-441-4	____	My Body, My Self for Girls	12.95pb	____
1-55704-440-6	____	My Body, My Self for Boys	12.95pb	____
1-55704-442-2	____	My Feelings, My Self	12.95pb	____
1-55704-414-7	____	Raising Your Jewish/Christian Child, Gruzen	16.95pb	____
1-55704-443-0	____	What's Happening to My Body?…Boys	12.95pb	____
1-55704-447-3	____	What's Happening to My Body?…Boys	22.95hc	____
1-55704-444-9	____	What's Happening to My Body?…Girls	12.95pb	____
1-55704-448-1	____	What's Happening to My Body?…Girls	22.95hc	____
1-55704-330-2	____	Your Child at Play: Birth to 1 Year, Segal	17.95pb	____
1-55704-334-5	____	Your Child at Play: Birth to 1 Year, Segal	27.95hc	____
1-55704-331-0	____	Your Child at Play: 1 to 2 Years, Segal	16.95pb	____
1-55704-335-3	____	Your Child at Play: 1 to 2 Years, Segal	27.95hc	____
1-55704-332-9	____	Your Child at Play: 2 to 3 Years, Segal	16.95pb	____
1-55704-336-1	____	Your Child at Play: 2 to 3 Years, Segal	27.95hc	____
1-55704-333-7	____	Your Child at Play: 3 to 5 Years, Segal	16.95pb	____
1-55704-337-X	____	Your Child at Play: 3 to 5 Years, Segal	27.95hc	____
1-55704-401-5	____	Your Child at Play: 5 to 8 Years, Segal	17.95pb	____
1-55704-402-3	____	Your Child at Play: 5 to 8 Years, Segal	29.95hc	____

*Shipping and Handling: Add $3.00 for the first item, and $1.00 for each additional item. For orders of 2 or more copies, call for special discount. Allow 4-6 weeks for delivery. Prices and availability are subject to change without notice.

Subtotal: $ _____

NY Residents add 8.25% State Sales Tax: $ _____

*Plus Shipping & Handling: $ _____

TOTAL AMOUNT ENCLOSED: $ _____